MEDITATIONS
ON MARY,
OUR MOTHER

St. John Henry Cardinal Newman

Cover & interior design by www.davidferrisdesign.com

Cover image: The Maesta, 1308-11 (tempera on panel), Duccio di Buoninsegna, (c.1278-1318) / Italian, Museo dell'Opera del Duomo, Siena, Italy/Bridgeman Images.
Cover & interior image: Cardinal Newman, from a photograph by Mr H. J. Whitlock, Look and Learn / Elgar Collection / Bridgeman Images.
Interior image: Mother of Perpetual Help, by Immaculate @ Shutterstock.com

LCCN: 2019950687

ISBN: 978-1-5051-1643-4
Published in the United States by
TAN Books
PO Box 410487
Charlotte, NC 28241
www.TANBooks.com
Printed in the United States of America

MEDITATIONS
ON MARY,
OUR MOTHER

St. John Henry Cardinal Newman

TAN Books
Gastonia, North Carolina

TABLE OF CONTENTS

EDITOR'S INTRODUCTION

St. John Henry Cardinal Newman's conversion to the Catholic Church in 1845 needs little by way of introduction. Most Catholics who know anything at all about Newman are familiar with his journey from Anglicanism to Rome. What may surprise them is the key role that devotion to the Blessed Virgin Mary played in that conversion.

Apart from the Papacy, devotion to Mary is perhaps the greatest stumbling block for the majority of Protestants. Yet, Newman had already developed a devotion to Mary and a defense of some Catholic doctrines on the subject even while he was still a Protestant. This requires some context.

In Newman's day, the "liberal" movement in theology was particularly strong. This liberalism rejected dogmatic principles as the basis of religion because they were independent of individual judgment. For early 19th century liberalism, the individual along with his interpretations and experiences was the standard of judgment in religion. In the early 20th century, this system of thought made its assault on the Catholic world, and received a new name: Modernism.

Nothing could be further from Cardinal Newman's thought, both as an Anglican and later in life as a Catholic. Newman's religion, as an Anglican, was based on the principle of dogma, that there are revealed truths to which the believer must adhere. These were the Holy Trinity, the Incarnation, Predestination, and the Lutheran hension of Christ (justification by faith). As time went on, Newman rejected the last, but he would remain steadfast with the first three throughout his life, even as a Catholic.

His acceptance of the Incarnation is the most important for his developing views on Mary. Christ became incarnate in time through a woman—who was this woman? Could she really be an insignificant figure? Moreover, as a student of history, Newman was well aware of early Christological controversies and early heresies in regard to the Incarnation. He was able to see clearly that they all received their death-blow when the Council of Ephesus had declared her to be *Theotokos*—Mother of God. The contrast in the Fathers between the old Eve and Mary as the new Eve made the matter quite clear, and served as a foundation for his developing and accepting further Marian doctrine, although he was still a Protestant. He even had no fear of proclaiming, as an Anglican minister, to his Anglican audience:

> Who can estimate the holiness and perfection of her, who was chosen to be the Mother of Christ? If to him that hath, more is given, and holiness and Divine favor go together (and this we are expressly told), what must have been the transcendent purity of her, whom the Creator Spirit condescended to overshadow with His miraculous presence? What must have been her gifts, who was chosen to be the only near earthly relative

of the Son of God, the only one whom He was bound by nature to revere and look up to; the one appointed to train and educate Him, to instruct Him day by day, as He grew in wisdom and in stature? This contemplation runs to a higher subject, did we dare follow it; for what, think you, was the sanctified state of that human nature, of which God formed His sinless Son; . . .? (*Parochial and Plain Sermons*, vol. ii, Sermon 12)

As his Marian doctrine and devotion grew, Newman ran up against a great road-block. In general, as the Tractarian controversy raged, and he was dissatisfied with the rejection of what he saw as historic Christianity by his own Church. He began to have a greater love, even longing for Rome, the mother of English Christianity. He felt, however, that whereas he had a logical, dogmatic based view of the Blessed Virgin Mary, Catholics went too far and said too much. Time, reading and prayer, however, would convince him otherwise, and he was able to say in his letter to the Anglo-Catholic Dr. Pusey (who had many of the same objections Newman once had):

Only this I know full well now, and did not know then, that the Catholic Church allows no image of any sort, material or immaterial, no dogmatic symbol, no rite, no sacrament, no Saint, not even the Blessed Virgin herself, to come between the soul and its Creator. It is face to face, "solus cum solo," in all matters between man and his God. He alone creates; He alone has redeemed; before His awful eyes we go in death; in the vision of Him is our eternal beatitude.

Thus, Newman's journey to the Church can said to have been guided by Our Lady, toward the kindly light which he was to rest in.

In honor of his canonization, this present volume draws together Newman's Marian writings into an anthology, and organizes them topically. We have drawn both from works that are doctrinal and apologetic, as well as devotional meditations, so as to show both sides of Newman's character. On the one hand, his profoundly logical, deep, and intellectual bearing, and on the other, the profound love that permeated his heart. Together, they show the great depths of Marian doctrine from the Church's treasury with which Newman has so powerfully permeated his own pages. In some places we have made minor edits for archaic language, as well as to tailor the readings for the purpose of this anthology.

—Gastonia, NC

Holy the womb that bore him,
Holy the breasts that fed,
But holier still the royal heart
That in His passion bled.

MARY THE
MOTHER OF GOD

MY SOUL DOTH
MAGNIFY THE LORD

The Angel began the salutation; he said, "Hail, thou that art highly favored;[1] the Lord is with thee; blessed art thou among women." Again, he said, "Fear not, Mary, for thou hast found favor with God; and, behold, thou shalt conceive in thy womb, and bring forth a Son, and shalt call His name Jesus. He shall be great, and shall be called the Son of the Highest." Her cousin Elizabeth was the next to greet her with her appropriate title. Though she was filled with the Holy Spirit at the time she spoke, yet, far from thinking herself by such a gift to be equal to Mary, she was thereby moved to use the lowlier and more reverent language. "She spoke out with a loud voice, and said, *Blessed art thou* among women, and blessed is the fruit of thy womb. And how is it that the mother of my Lord should come to me?" ... Then she repeated, "Blessed is she that believed; for there shall be a performance of those things which were told her from the Lord."

Then it was that Mary expressed her feelings in the *Magnificat* we read in the Evening Service. How many and complicated must they have been! In her was now to be fulfilled that promise which the world had been looking out for during thousands of years. The Seed of the woman, announced to guilty Eve, after long delay, was at length appearing upon earth, and was to be born of her. In her the destinies of the world were to be reversed, and the serpent's head bruised. On her was bestowed the greatest

2

honor ever put upon any individual of our fallen race. God was taking upon Him her flesh, and humbling Himself to be called her offspring;—such is the deep mystery! She of course would feel her own inexpressible unworthiness; and again, her humble lot, and her weakness in the eyes of the world. And she had moreover, that purity and innocence of heart, that bright vision of faith, that confiding trust in her God, which raised all these feelings to an intensity which we, ordinary mortals, cannot understand. *We* cannot understand them; we repeat her hymn day after day—yet consider for an instant how differently *we* say it from how she first uttered it. *We* even hurry it over, and do not think of the meaning of those words which came from the most highly favored, awfully gifted of the children of men. "My soul doth magnify the Lord, and my spirit hath rejoiced in God my Savior. For He hath regarded the low estate of His hand-maiden: for, behold, from henceforth all generations shall call me blessed. For He that is mighty hath done to me great things; and holy is His name. And His mercy is on them that fear Him from generation to generation."

– Parochial and Plain Sermons, II

MOTHER OF THE CREATOR

This is a title which, of all others, we should have thought it impossible for any creature to possess. At first sight we might be tempted to say that it throws into confusion our primary ideas of the Creator and the creature, the Eternal and the temporal, the Self-subsisting and the dependent; and yet on further consideration we shall see that we cannot refuse the title to Mary without denying the Divine Incarnation—that is, the great and fundamental truth of revelation, that God became man.

And this was seen from the first age of the Church. Christians were accustomed from the first to call the Blessed Virgin "The Mother of God," because they saw that it was impossible to deny her that title without denying St. John's words, "The Word" (that is, God the Son) "was made flesh."

And in no long time it was found necessary to proclaim this truth by the voice of an Ecumenical Council of the Church. For, in consequence of the dislike which men have of a mystery, the error sprang up that our Lord was not really God, but a man, differing from us in this merely—that God dwelt in Him, as God dwells in all good men, only in a higher measure; as the Holy Spirit dwelt in Angels and Prophets, as in a sort of Temple; or again, as our Lord now dwells in the Tabernacle in church. And then the bishops and faithful people found there was no other way of hindering this false, bad view being taught but by declaring distinctly, and making it a point of faith, that Mary was the Mother, not of man only, but of God. And since that time the title of Mary, as *Mother of God*, has become what is called a dogma, or article of faith, in the Church.

But this leads us to a larger view of the subject. Is this title as given to Mary more wonderful than the doctrine that God, without ceasing to be God, should become man? Is it more mysterious that Mary should be Mother of God, than that *God* should be *man*? Yet the latter, as I have said, is the elementary truth of revelation, witnessed by Prophets, Evangelists, and Apostles all through Scripture. And what can be more consoling and joyful than the wonderful promises which follow from this truth, that Mary is the Mother of God?—the great wonder, namely, that we become the brethren of our God! That, if we live well, and die in the grace of God, we shall all of us hereafter be taken up by our Incarnate God to that place where angels dwell! That our bodies shall be raised from the dust, and be taken to Heaven; that we shall be really united to God; that we shall be partakers of the Divine nature; that each of us, soul and body, shall be plunged into the abyss of glory which surrounds the Almighty; that we shall see Him, and share His blessedness, according to the text, "Whosoever shall do the will of My Father that is in Heaven, the same is My brother, and sister, and mother."

−Meditations on the Litany of Loretto
for the Month of May

THE HIDDEN MOTHER

Now, when we turn to the Gospels, I think everyone must feel some surprise that we are not told more about the Blessed Virgin than we find there. After the circumstances of Christ's birth and infancy, we hear little of her. Little is said in praise of her. She is mentioned as attending Christ to the cross, and there committed by Him to St. John's keeping, and she is mentioned as continuing with the Apostles in prayer after His ascension. Then we hear no more of her. But here again in this silence we find instruction, as much as in the mention of her.

It suggests to us that Scripture was written, not to exalt this or that particular Saint, but to give glory to Almighty God. There have been thousands of holy souls in the times of which the Biblical history treats, whom we know nothing of, because their lives did not fall upon the line of God's public dealings with man. In Scripture we read not of all the good men who ever were, only of a few, viz. those in whom God's name was especially honored. Doubtless there have been many widows in Israel, serving God in fasting and prayer, like Anna. Yet, she alone is mentioned in Scripture, as being in a situation to glorify the Lord Jesus. She spoke of the Infant Savior "to all them that looked for redemption in Jerusalem." Nay, for what we know, faith like Abraham's, and zeal like David's, have burned in the breasts of thousands whose names have no memorial; because, I say, Scripture is written to show us the course of God's great and marvelous providence, and

6

we hear of those Saints only who were the instruments of His purposes, as either introducing or preaching His Son.

Christ's favored Apostle was St. John, His personal friend. But how little do we know of St. John compared with St. Paul—and why? because St. Paul was the more illustrious propagator and dispenser of His Truth. As St. Paul himself said, that he "knew no man after the flesh," (2 Cor. 5:16), so His Savior, with somewhat a similar meaning, has hid from us the knowledge of His more sacred and familiar feelings, His feelings towards His Mother and His friend.

When a Saint is seen working *towards* an end appointed by God, we *see* him to be a mere instrument, a servant though a favored one; and though we admire him, yet, after all, we glorify God in him. We pass on *from* him to the work to which he ministers. But, when anyone is introduced, full of gifts, yet without visible and immediate obedience to God's designs, such a one seems revealed for his own sake.

Therefore, many truths are, like the "things which the seven thunders uttered," (Rev. 10:4). "sealed up" from us. In particular, it is in mercy to us that so little is revealed about the Blessed Virgin, in mercy to our weakness, though of her there are "many things to say," yet they are "hard to be uttered, seeing we are dull of hearing" (Heb. 5:11).

Other saints are but influenced or inspired by Christ, and made partakers of Him mystically. But, as to St. Mary, Christ derived His manhood from her, and so had an especial unity of nature with her. For, truly, she is raised above the condition of sinful beings; she is brought near to God, yet is but a creature. Hence, following the example of Scripture, we had better only think of her with and for her Son, never separating her from Him, but using her name as a memorial of His great condescension in stooping from heaven, and not "abhorring the Virgin's womb." And, with this caution, the thought of her may be made most profitable to our faith; for nothing is so calculated to impress on our minds that Christ is really partaker of our nature, and in all respects man, save sin only, as to associate Him with the thought of her, by whose ministration He became our brother.

—Parochial and Plain Sermons, II

DESTROYER OF HERESIES

I have said that there was in the first ages no public and ecclesiastical recognition of the place which Our Lady holds in the economy of grace. This was reserved for the fifth century, just as the definition of our Lord's proper Divinity had been the work of the fourth. There was a controversy contemporary with earlier heresies, I mean the Nestorian, which brought out the complement of the development, which they had inadvertently served to bring about. If I may so speak, they supplied the subject of the august proposition of which Arianism had provided the predicate. In order to honor Christ, in order to defend the true doctrine of the Incarnation, in order to secure a right faith in the humanity of the Eternal Son, the Council of Ephesus determined the Blessed Virgin to be the Mother of God. Thus, all heresies of that day, though opposite to each other, in a most wonderful way were the cause of her exaltation.

The spontaneous or traditional feeling of Christians had in great measure anticipated the formal ecclesiastical decision. Thus, the title *Theotokos*, or Mother of God, was familiar to Christians from primitive times, and had been used, among other writers, by Origen, Eusebius, St. Alexander, St. Athanasius, St. Ambrose, St. Gregory Nazianzen, St. Gregory Nyssen, and St. Nilus. She had been called Ever-Virgin by others, as by St. Epiphanius, St. Jerome, and Didymus. By others, "the Mother of all living," as being the antitype of Eve; for, as St. Epiphanius observes, "in truth," not in shadow, "from Mary was Life itself brought into the world, that Mary might bear things living, and might become Mother of living things." St. Augustine says that all have sinned "except the Holy Virgin Mary, concerning whom, for the honor of the Lord, I wish no question to be raised at all, when we are treating of sins." "She was alone and wrought the world's salvation," says St. Ambrose, alluding to her conception of the Redeemer. She is signified by the Pillar of the cloud which guided the Israelites, according to the same Father; and she had "so great grace, as not only to have virginity herself, but to impart it to those to whom she came;"— "the Rod out of the stem of Jesse," says St. Jerome, and "the Eastern gate through which the High Priest alone goes in and out, yet is ever shut;"—the wise woman, says St. Nilus, who "hath clad all believers, from the fleece of the Lamb born of her, with the clothing of incorruption, and delivered them from their spiritual nakedness;"— "the Mother of Life, of beauty, of majesty, the Morning Star," according to Antiochus;— "the mystical new heavens," "the heavens carrying the Divinity," "the fruitful vine by whom we are carried from death unto life," according to St. Ephraim;— "the manna which is delicate, bright, sweet, and virgin, which, as though coming from heaven, has poured down on all the people of the Churches a food pleasanter than honey," according to St. Maximus.

St. Proclus calls her "the unsullied shell which contains the pearl of price," "the sacred shrine of sinlessness," "the golden altar of holocaust," "the holy oil of anointing," "the costly alabaster box of spikenard," "the ark gilt within and without," "the heifer whose ashes, that is, the Lord's Body taken from her, cleanses those who are defiled by the pollution of sin," "the fair bride of the Canticles," "the stay (*sterigma*) of believers," "the Church's crown," "the expression of orthodoxy." These are oratorical expressions; but we use oratory on great subjects, not on small. Elsewhere he calls her "God's only bridge to man;" and elsewhere he breaks forth, "Run through all creation in your thoughts, and see if there be equal to, or greater than, the Holy Virgin Mother of God."

—Essay on the Development of Doctrine

SORROWFUL MOTHER

The special name by which our Lord was known before His coming was that of Messiah, or Christ. Thus, He was known to the Jews. But when He actually showed Himself on earth, He was known by three new titles, the Son of God, the Son of Man, and the Savior; the first expressive of His Divine Nature, the second of His Human, the third of His Personal Office. The Angel who appeared to Mary called Him the Son of God; the angel who appeared to Joseph called Him *Jesus*, which means in English, *Savior*; and so, the Angels also called Him a Savior when they appeared to the shepherds. But He Himself specially calls Himself the Son of Man.

Not Angels only call Him Savior, but those two greatest of the Apostles, Sts. Peter and Paul, in their first preachings. St. Peter says He is "a Prince and a Savior," and St. Paul says, "a Savior, Jesus." And both Angels and Apostles tell us why He is so called—because He has rescued us from the power of the evil spirit, and from the guilt and misery of our sins. This is why the Angel says to Joseph, "Thou shalt call His name Jesus, *for* He shall save His people from their *sins*;" and St. Peter, "God has exalted Him to be Prince and Savior, to give repentance to Israel, and remission of sins." And He says Himself, "The Son of Man is come to seek and to *save that which is lost*."

Now let us consider how this affects our thoughts of Mary. To rescue slaves from the power of the Enemy implies a conflict. Our Lord, because He was a Savior, was

12

a warrior. He could not deliver the captives without a fight, nor without personal suffering. Now, who are they who especially hate wars? A pagan poet answers. "Wars," he says, "are hated by *Mothers*." Mothers are just those who especially suffer in a war. They may glory in the honor gained by their children; but still such glorying does not wipe out one particle of the long pain, the anxiety, the suspense, the desolation, and the anguish which the mother of a soldier feels.

So it was with Mary. For thirty years she was blessed with the continual presence of her Son—nay, she had Him in subjection. But the time came when that war for which He had come upon earth called for Him. Certainly, He came, not simply to be the Son of Mary, but to be the Savior of Man, and at length He parted from her. She knew *then* what it was to be the mother of a soldier. He left her side; she saw Him no longer; she tried in vain to get near Him. He had for years lived in her embrace, and after that, at least in her dwelling—but now, in His own words, "The Son of Man had not where to lay His head." And then, when years had run out, she heard of His arrest, His mock trial, and His passion. At last she got near Him— when and where?—on the way to Calvary. And when He had been lifted upon the Cross. And at length she held Him again in her arms: yes—when He was dead. True, He rose from the dead; but still she did not thereby gain Him, for He ascended on high, and she did not at once follow Him. No, she remained on earth many years—in the care, indeed, of His dearest Apostle, St. John. But what

13

was even the holiest of men compared with her own Son, and Him the Son of God? O Holy Mary, Mother of our Savior, in this meditation we have now suddenly passed from the Joyful Mysteries to the Sorrowful, from Gabriel's Annunciation to thee, to the Seven Dolors. That, then, will be the next series of Meditations which we make about thee.

—Meditations on the Litany of Loretto
for the Month of May

MARY, THE
SECOND EVE

CHANGING EVA'S NAME

What is the great rudimental teaching of Antiquity from its earliest date concerning her? By "rudimental teaching," I mean the *primâ facie* view of her person and office, the broad outline laid down of her, the aspect under which she comes to us, in the writings of the Fathers. She is the Second Eve. Now let us consider what this implies. Eve had a definite, essential position in the First Covenant. The fate of the human race lay with Adam; he it was who represented us. It was in Adam that we fell. Although Eve had fallen, still, if Adam had stood, we should not have lost those supernatural privileges which were bestowed upon him as our first father. Yet though Eve was not the head of the race, still, even as regards the race, she had a place of her own; for Adam, to whom was divinely committed the naming of all things, named her "the Mother of all the living," a name surely expressive, not of a fact only, but of a dignity. But further, as she thus had her own general relation to the human race, so again had she her own special place, as regards its trial and its fall in Adam.

In those primeval events, Eve had an integral share. "The woman, being seduced, was in the transgression." She listened to the Evil Angel; she offered the fruit to her husband, and he ate of it. She co-operated, not as an irresponsible instrument, but intimately and personally in the sin: she brought it about. As the history stands, she was a *sine-quanon*, a positive, active, cause of it. And she had her share in its punishment. In the sentence pronounced on her, she was

16

recognized as a real agent in the temptation and its issue, and she suffered accordingly. In that awful transaction there were three parties concerned,—the serpent, the woman, and the man. At the time of their sentence, an event was announced for a distant future, in which the three same parties were to meet again, the serpent, the woman, and the man; but it was to be a second Adam and a second Eve, and the new Eve was to be the mother of the new Adam. "I will put enmity between thee and the woman, and between thy seed and her seed." The Seed of the woman is the Word Incarnate, and the Woman, whose seed or son He is, is His mother Mary. This interpretation, and the parallelism it involves, seem to me undeniable; but at all events (and this is my point) the parallelism is the doctrine of the Fathers, from the earliest times; and, this being established, we are able, by the position and office of Eve in our fall, to determine the position and office of Mary in our restoration.

As St. Irenaeus says, "With a fitness, Mary the Virgin is found obedient, saying, 'Behold Thy handmaid, O Lord; be it to me according to Thy word.' But Eve was disobedient; for she obeyed not, while she was yet a virgin. As she, having indeed Adam for a husband, but as yet being a virgin ... becoming disobedient, became the cause of death both to herself and to the whole human race, so also Mary, having the predestined man, and being yet a Virgin, being obedient, became both to herself and to the whole human race the cause of salvation ... And on account of this the Lord said, that the first should be last and the last first."

–Letter to Dr. Pusey

COOPERATOR IN
OUR REDEMPTION

Among the Fathers who write about the Blessed Virgin what is immediately noticeable is that they do not speak of her merely as the physical instrument of our Lord's taking flesh, but as an intelligent, responsible cause of it. Her faith and obedience were accessories to the Incarnation, and gaining it as her reward. As Eve failed in these virtues, and thereby brought on the fall of the race in Adam, so Mary by means of the same had a part in its restoration. Some might say that the Blessed Virgin was only a physical instrument of our redemption; "what has been said of her by the Fathers as the chosen *vessel* of the Incarnation, was applied *personally* to her," (that is, by Catholics,) and again "the Fathers speak of the Blessed Virgin as the *instrument* of our salvation, *in that* she gave birth to the Redeemer."

On the other hand, St. Augustine, in well-known passages, speaks of her as more exalted by her sanctity than by her relationship to our Lord. However, not to go beyond the doctrine of Justin, Irenaeus and Tertullian, they unanimously declare that she was *not* a mere instrument in the Incarnation, such as David, or Judah, may be considered. They declare she co-operated in our salvation not merely by the descent of the Holy Spirit upon her body, but by specific holy acts, the effect of the Holy Spirit within her soul. Moreover, as Eve forfeited privileges by sin, so Mary earned privileges by the fruits of grace. As

18

Eve was disobedient and unbelieving, so Mary was obedient and believing. Then, as Eve was a cause of ruin to all, Mary was a cause of salvation to all; Eve made room for Adam's fall, so Mary made room for our Lord's reparation of it. Thus, whereas the free gift was not as the offence, but much greater, it follows that, as Eve co-operated in effecting a great evil, Mary co-operated in effecting a much greater good.

And, besides the run of the argument, which reminds the reader of St. Paul's antithetical sentences in tracing the analogy between Adam's work and our Lord's work, it is well to observe the particular words under which the Blessed Virgin's office is described. Tertullian says that Mary "blotted out" Eve's fault, and "brought back the female sex," or "the human race, to salvation;" and St. Irenæus says that "by obedience she was the cause or occasion of salvation to herself and the whole human race;" that by her the human race is saved; that by her Eve's complication is disentangled; and that she is Eve's Advocate, or friend in need. It is supposed by critics, Protestant as well as Catholic, that the Greek word for Advocate in the original was Paraclete; it should be borne in mind, then, when we are accused of giving our Lady the titles and offices of her Son, that St. Irenæus bestows on her the special Name and Office proper to the Holy Spirit.

—*Letter to Dr. Pusey*

THE MAN, THE SERPENT, AND THE WOMAN

The special prerogatives of St. Mary, the *Virgo Virginum*, are intimately involved in the doctrine of the Incarnation itself, with which these remarks began, and have already been dwelt upon above. As is well known, they were not fully recognized in the Catholic ritual till a late date, but they were not a new thing in the Church, or strange to her earlier teachers. St. Justin, St. Irenæus, and others, had distinctly laid it down, that she not only had an office, but bore a part, and was a voluntary agent, in the actual process of redemption, as Eve had been instrumental and responsible in Adam's fall. They taught that, as the first woman might have foiled the Tempter and did not, so, if Mary had been disobedient or unbelieving on Gabriel's message, the Divine Economy would have been frustrated. And certainly, the parallel between "the Mother of all living" and the Mother of the Redeemer may be gathered from a comparison of the first chapters of Scripture with the last.

It was noticed in another place, that the only passage where the serpent is directly identified with the evil spirit occurs in the twelfth chapter of the Revelation; now it is observable that the recognition, when made, is found in the course of a vision of a "woman clothed with the sun and the moon under her feet:" thus two women are brought into contrast with each other. Moreover, as it is said in the Apocalypse, "The dragon was wroth with the woman, and went about to make war with the remnant of her seed," so is it prophesied in Genesis, "I will put enmity between thee and the woman, and between thy seed and her Seed. He shall bruise thy head, and thou shalt bruise His heel." Also the enmity was to exist, not only between the Serpent and the Seed of the woman, but between the serpent and the woman herself; and here too there is a correspondence in the Apocalyptic vision. If then there is reason for thinking that this mystery at the close of the Scripture record answers to the mystery in the beginning of it, and that "the Woman" mentioned in both passages is one and the same, then she can be none other than St. Mary, thus introduced prophetically to our notice immediately on the transgression of Eve.

Here, however, we are not so much concerned to interpret Scripture as to examine the Fathers. Thus St. Justin says, "Eve, being a virgin and incorrupt, having conceived the word from the Serpent, bore disobedience and death; but Mary the Virgin, receiving faith and joy, when Gabriel the Angel evangelized her, answered, 'Be it unto me according to thy word.'" And Tertullian says that, whereas Eve believed the Serpent, and Mary believed Gabriel, "the fault of Eve in believing, Mary by believing hath blotted out." St. Irenæus speaks more explicitly: "As Eve," he says ... "becoming disobedient, became the cause of death to herself and to all mankind, so Mary too, having the predestined Man, and yet a Virgin, being obedient, became cause of salvation both to herself and to all mankind." This becomes the received doctrine in the Post-nicene Church.

—Essay on the Development of Doctrine

GATE OF HEAVEN

Mary is called the *Gate* of Heaven, because it was through her that our Lord passed from heaven to earth. The Prophet Ezechiel, prophesying of Mary, says, "the gate shall be closed, it shall not be opened, and no man shall pass through it, since the Lord God of Israel has entered through it—and it shall be closed for the Prince, the Prince Himself shall sit in it."

Now this is fulfilled, not only in our Lord having taken flesh from her, and being her Son, but, moreover, in that she had a place in the economy of Redemption; it is fulfilled in her spirit and will, as well as in her body. Eve had a part in the fall of man, though it was Adam who was our representative, and whose sin made us sinners. It was Eve who began, and who tempted Adam. Scripture says: "The woman saw that the tree was good to eat, and fair to the eyes, and delightful to behold; and she took of the fruit thereof, and did eat, and gave to her husband, and he did eat." It was fitting then in God's mercy that, as the woman began the *destruction* of the world, so woman should also begin its *recovery*, and that, as Eve opened the way for the fatal deed of the first Adam, so Mary should open the way for the great achievement of the second Adam, even our Lord Jesus Christ, who came to save the world by dying on the cross for it. Hence Mary is called by the holy Fathers a second and a better Eve, as having taken that first step in the salvation of mankind which Eve took in its ruin.

How, and when, did Mary take part, and the initial part, in the world's restoration? It was when the Angel

Gabriel came to her to announce to her the great dignity which was to be her portion. St. Paul bids us "present our bodies to God as a reasonable service." We must not only pray with our lips, and fast, and do outward penance, and be chaste in our bodies; but we must be obedient, and pure in our minds. And so, as regards the Blessed Virgin, it was God's will that she should undertake *willingly* and with *full understanding* to be the Mother of our Lord, and not to be a mere passive instrument whose maternity would have no merit and no reward. The higher our gifts, the heavier our duties. It was no light lot to be so intimately near to the Redeemer of men, as she experienced afterwards when she suffered with him. Therefore, weighing well the Angel's words before giving her answer to them—first she asked whether so great an office would be a forfeiture of that Virginity which she had vowed. When the Angel told her no, then, with the full consent of a full heart, full of God's love to her and her own lowliness, she said, "Behold the handmaid of the Lord; be it done unto me according to thy word." It was by this consent that she became the *Gate of Heaven*.

—Meditations for the Month of May

EVER-VIRGIN

MOTHER OF CHRIST

Each of the titles of Mary has its own special meaning and drift, and may be made the subject of a distinct meditation. She is invoked by us as the *Mother of Christ*. We address her in this way to bring before us that she it is who from the first was prophesied of, and associated with the hopes and prayers of all holy men, of all true worshipers of God, of all who "looked for the redemption of Israel" in every age before that redemption came.

Our Lord was called the Christ, or the Messiah, by the Jewish prophets and the Jewish people. The two words Christ and Messiah mean the same. They mean in English the "Anointed." In the old time there were three great ministries, or offices, by means of which God spoke to His chosen people, the Israelites, or, as they were afterward called, the Jews, viz., that of Priest, that of King, and that of Prophet. Those who were chosen by God for one or other of these offices were solemnly anointed with oil—oil signifying the grace of God, which was given to them for the due performance of their high duties. But our Lord was all three, a Priest, a Prophet, and a King—a Priest, because He offered Himself as a sacrifice for our sins; a Prophet, because He revealed to us the Holy Law of God; and a King, because He rules over us. Thus, He is the one true Christ.

It was in expectation of this great Messiah that the chosen people, the Jews, or Israelites, or Hebrews (for these are different names for the same people), looked out from age to age. He was to come to set all things right. And next to this great question which occupied their minds, namely, *When* was He to come, was the question, *Who* was to be His Mother? It had been told them from the first, not that He should come from heaven, but that He should be born of a Woman. At the time of the fall of Adam, God had said that the *seed* of the *Woman* should bruise the Serpent's head. At the end of many centuries, it was further revealed to the Jews that the great Messiah, or Christ, the seed of the Woman, should be born of their race, and of one particular tribe of the twelve tribes into which that race was divided. It stood to reason, since He was so great, the Mother must be great, and good, and blessed too. Hence it was, among other reasons, that they thought so highly of the marriage state, because, not knowing the mystery of the miraculous conception of the Christ when He was actually to come, they thought that the marriage rite was the ordinance necessary for His coming.

Hence it was, if Mary had been as other women, she would have longed for marriage, as opening on her the prospect of bearing the great King. But she was too humble and too pure for such thoughts. She had been inspired to choose that better way of serving God which had not been made known to the Jews—the state of Virginity. She preferred to be His Spouse to being His Mother. Accordingly, when the Angel Gabriel announced to her that high destiny, she shrank from it till she was assured that it would not oblige her to revoke her purpose of a virgin life devoted to her God.

Thus was it that she became the Mother of the Christ, not in that way which pious women for so many ages had expected Him, but, declining the grace of such maternity, she gained it by means of a higher graces And this is the full meaning of St. Elizabeth's words, when the Blessed Virgin came to Visit her, which we use in the Hail Mary: "Blessed art thou among women, and blessed is the fruit of thy womb." And therefore, it is that in the Devotion called the "*Crown of Twelve Stars*" we give praise to God the Holy Spirit, through whom she was *both* Virgin *and* Mother.

–Meditations on the Litany of Loretto
for the Month of May

HE OPENS AND NOBODY CLOSES

Since He was the All-holy Son of God, though He con-descended to be born into the world, He necessarily came into it in a way suitable to the All-holy, and differ-ent from that of other men. He took our nature upon Him, but not our sin; taking our nature in a way above nature. Did He then come from heaven in the clouds? did He frame a body for Himself out of the dust of the earth? No; He was, as other men, "made of a woman," as St. Paul speaks, that He might take on Him, not another nature, but the nature of man. It had been prophesied from the beginning, that the Seed of the woman should bruise the serpent's head. "I will put enmity," said Almighty God to the serpent at the fall, "between thee and the woman, and between thy seed and her Seed; It shall bruise thy head." (Gen. 3:15). In consequence of this promise, pious women, we are told, were in the old time ever looking out in hope that in their own instance, the promise might find its accomplishment. One after another hoped in turn that she herself might be mother of the promised King; and therefore marriage was in repute, and virginity in dis-esteem, as if then only they had a prospect of being the Mother of Christ, if they waited for the blessing according to the course of nature, and amid the generations of men. Pious women they were, but little understanding the real condition of mankind.

It was ordained, indeed, that the Eternal Word should come into the world by the ministration of a woman; but born in the way of the flesh He could not be. Mankind is a fallen race; ever since the Fall there has been a "fault and corruption of the nature of every man that naturally is engendered of the offspring of Adam; ... so that the flesh lusts always contrary to the Spirit, and therefore in every person born into this world it deserves God's wrath and damnation." And "the Apostle doth confess that concupiscence and lust hath of itself the nature of sin." "That which is born of the flesh, is flesh." "Who can bring a clean thing out of an unclean?" "How can he be clean that is born of a woman?" Or as holy David cries out, "Behold, I was conceived in wickedness, and in sin hath my mother conceived me." (John 3:6. Job 14:4; 25:4. Ps. 51:5). No one is born into the world without sin; or can rid himself of the sin of his birth except by a second birth through the Spirit. How then could the Son of God have come as a Holy Savior, had He come as other men? How could He have atoned for our sins, who Himself had guilt? or cleansed our hearts, who was impure Himself? or raised up our heads, who was Himself the son of shame? Surely any such messenger had needed a Savior for his own disease, and to such a one would apply the proverb, "Physician, heal thyself." Priests among men are they who have to offer "first for their own sins, and then for the people's;" (Heb. 7:27) but He, coming as the immaculate Lamb of God, and the all-prevailing Priest, could not come in the way which those fond persons anticipated. He came by a new and living way, by which He alone has come, and which alone became Him. The Prophet Isaiah had been the first to announce it: "The Lord Himself shall give you a sign," he says, "Behold, a Virgin shall conceive and bear a Son, and shall call His Name Immanuel." And accordingly, St. Matthew after quoting this text, declares its fulfilment in the instance of the Blessed Mary. "All this," he says, "was done that it might be fulfilled which was spoken by the prophet."

—Parochial and Plain Sermons, V

MADE KNOWN BY THE
MESSAGE OF AN ANGEL

Two separate Angels, one to Mary, one to Joseph, declare who the adorable Agent was, by whom this miracle was wrought. "Joseph, thou son of David," an Angel said to him, "fear not to take unto thee Mary thy wife, for that which is conceived in her is of the Holy Spirit;" and what followed from this? He proceeds, "And she shall bring forth a Son, and thou shalt call His Name Jesus, for He shall save His people from their sins." Because He was "incarnate by the Holy Spirit of the Virgin Mary," therefore He was "Jesus," a "Savior from sin." Again, the Angel Gabriel had already said to Mary, "Hail, full of Grace, the Lord is with thee: blessed art thou among women." And then he proceeds to declare that her Son should be called Jesus; that He "should be great, and should be called the Son of the Highest;" and that "of His Kingdom there shall be no end." And he concludes by announcing, "The Holy Spirit shall come upon thee, and the power of the Highest shall overshadow thee; therefore, that Holy Thing which shall be born of thee shall be called the Son of God." (Matt. 1:20, 21. Luke 1:28-35). Because God the Holy Spirit wrought miraculously, therefore was her Son a "Holy Thing," "the Son of God," and "Jesus," and the heir of an everlasting kingdom.

This is the great Mystery which we are now celebrating, of which mercy is the beginning, and sanctity the end: according to the Psalm, "Righteousness and peace have kissed each other." He who is all purity came to an impure race to raise them to His purity. He, the brightness of God's glory, came in a body of flesh, which was pure and holy as Himself, "without spot, or wrinkle, or any such thing, but holy and without blemish;" and this He did for our sake, "that we might be partakers of His holiness." He needed not a human nature for Himself— He was all-perfect in His original Divine nature; but He took upon Himself what was ours for the sake of us. He who "hath made of one blood all nations of men," so that in the sin of one all sinned, and in the death of one all died, He came in that very nature of Adam, in order to communicate to us that nature as it is in His Person, that "our sinful bodies might be made clean by His Body, and our souls washed through His most precious Blood;" to make us partakers of the Divine nature; to sow the seed of eternal life in our hearts; and to raise us from "the corruption that is in the world through lust," to that immaculate purity and that fulness of grace which is in Him. He who is the first principle and pattern of all things, came to be the beginning and pattern of human kind, the first-born of the whole creation. He, who is the everlasting Light, became the Light of men; He, who is the Life from eternity, became the Life of a race dead in sin; He, who is the Word of God, came to be a spiritual Word, "dwelling richly in our hearts," an "engrafted Word, which is able to save our souls;" He, who is the co-equal Son of the Father, came to be the Son of God in our flesh, that He might raise us also to the adoption of sons, and might be first among many brethren. And this is the reason why the Collect for the season, after speaking of our Lord as the Only-begotten Son, and born in our nature of a pure Virgin, proceeds to speak of our new birth and adopted sonship, and renewal by the grace of the Holy Spirit.

—Parochial and Plain Sermons, V

SHE KEPT ALL THINGS
IN HER HEART

Let those who deny that the Son is from the Father by nature and proper to His substance, deny also that He took true human flesh of Mary Ever-Virgin. —St. Athanasius

I have said in a note on the word in the *Aurea Catena*, that the word "till" need not imply a termination at a certain point of time, but may be given as information up to a certain point from which onwards there is already no doubt. Supposing an Evangelist thought the very notion shocking that Joseph should have considered the Blessed Virgin as his wife, *after* he was witness of her bearing the Son of God, he would only say that the vision had its effect upon him up to that date, when the idea was monstrous. If one said of a profligate, that, in consequence of some awful warning, he had said a prayer for grace every night up to the time of his conversion, no one would gather thence that he left off praying on being converted. "Michal the daughter of Saul had no child *to* the day of her death;" had she children after it? …

It is at first strange that these instances of special exemptions should be named by early writers, without our Lady also being mentioned; or rather it would be strange, unless we bore in mind how little is said of her at all by Scripture or the Fathers up to the Council of Ephesus, A.D. 431. It would seem as if, till our Lord's glory called for it, it required an effort for the reverent devotion of the Church to speak much about her or to make her the subject of popular preaching; but, when by her manifestation a right faith in her Divine Son was to be secured, then the Church was to be guided in a contrary course. It must be recollected that there was a *disciplina arcani* in the first centuries, and, if it was exercised, as far as might be, as regards the Holy Trinity and the Eucharist, so would it be as regards the Blessed Virgin.

The meaning and practical results of deep-seated religious reverence were far better understood in the primitive times than now, when the infidelity of the world has corrupted the Church. Now, we allow ourselves publicly to canvass the most solemn truths in a careless or fiercely argumentative way. Truths, which it is as useless as it is unseemly to discuss before men, as being attainable only by the sober and watchful, by slow degrees, with dependence on the Giver of wisdom, and with strict obedience to the light which has already been granted. Then, they would scarcely express in writing, what now is not only preached to the mixed crowds who frequent our churches, but circulated in prints among all ranks and classes of the unclean and the profane, and pressed upon all who choose to purchase. Nay, so perplexed is the present state of things, that *the Church is obliged to change her course of acting*, after the spirit of the alteration made at Nicæa, and unwillingly to take part in the theological discussions of the day, as a man crushes venomous creatures of necessity, powerful to do it, but loathing the employment. ...

The silence of Scripture about the Blessed Virgin in

its narrative of the Resurrection is illustrative. "Here perhaps," I say, "we learn a lesson from the deep silence which Scripture observes concerning the Blessed Virgin after the Resurrection; as if she, who was too pure and holy a flower to be more than seen here on earth, even during the season of her Son's humiliation, was altogether drawn by the Angels into paradise on His Resurrection."

—Select Treatises of St. Athanasius, vol. II.

THE MOST DEVOUT VIRGIN

To be *devout* is to be devoted. We know what is meant by a devoted wife or daughter. It is one whose thoughts center in the person so deeply loved, so tenderly cherished. She follows him about with her eyes; she is ever seeking some means of serving him; and, if her services are very small in their character, that only shows how intimate they are, and how incessant. And especially if the object of her love be weak, or in pain, or near to die, still more intensely does she live in his life, and know nothing but him.

This intense devotion towards our Lord, forgetting self in love for Him, is instanced in St. Paul, who says, "I know nothing but Jesus Christ and Him crucified." And again, "I live, [yet] now not I, but Christ lives in me; and [the life] that I now live in the flesh, I live in the faith of the Son of God, who loved me, and delivered Himself for me."

But great as was St. Paul's devotion to our Lord, much greater was that of the Blessed Virgin; because she was His Mother, and because she had Him and all His sufferings actually before her eyes, and because she had the long intimacy of thirty years with Him, and because she was from her special sanctity so ineffably near to Him in spirit. When, then, He was mocked, bruised, scourged, and nailed to the Cross, she felt as keenly as if every indignity and torture inflicted on Him was struck at herself. She could have cried out in agony at every pang of His.

To be devout is also to be a martyr. She was a martyr

without the rude dishonor that accompanied the sufferings of martyrs. The martyrs were seized, haled about, thrust into prison with the vilest criminals, and assailed with the most blasphemous and foulest speeches that Satan could inspire. Our Lord was buffeted, stripped, scourged, mocked, dragged about, and then stretched, nailed, lifted up on a high cross, to the gaze of a brutal multitude.

But He, who bore the sinner's shame for sinners, spared His mother, who was sinless, the supreme indignity. Not in the body, but in the soul, she suffered. In His Agony she was agonized; in His passion she suffered a like-passion; she was crucified with Him; the spear that pierced His chest pierced through her spirit. Yet there were no visible signs of this intimate martyrdom; she stood up, still, collected, motionless, solitary, under the Cross of her Son, surrounded by Angels, and shrouded in her virginal sanctity from the notice of all who were taking part in His crucifixion.

—*Meditations on the Litany of Loretto*
for the Month of May

THE DIGNITY
OF MARY

ALL GENERATIONS
SHALL CALL ME BLESSED

Now, her dignity. Here let us suppose that our first parents had overcome in their trial; and had gained for their descendants forever the full possession, as if by right, of the privileges which were promised to their obedience—grace here and glory hereafter. Is it possible that those descendants, pious and happy from age to age in their temporal homes, would have forgotten their benefactors? Would they not have followed them in thought into the heavens, and gratefully commemorated them on earth? The history of the temptation, the craft of the serpent, their steadfastness in obedience—the loyal vigilance, the sensitive purity of Eve—the great issue, salvation wrought out for all generations—would have been never from their minds, ever welcome to their ears. This would have taken place from the necessity of our nature. Every nation has its mythical hymns and epics about its first fathers and its heroes. The great deeds of Charlemagne, Alfred, Coeur de Lion, Louis IX, Wallace, Joan of Arc, do not die. Although their persons are gone from us, we make much of their names. Milton's Adam, after his fall, understands the force of this law and shrinks from the prospect of its operation.

"Who of all ages to succeed, but, feeling
   The evil on him brought by me, will curse
   My head? Ill fare our ancestor impure,
   For this we may thank Adam."

If this anticipation of the first man has not been fulfilled in the event, it is owing to the exigencies of our penal life, our state of perpetual change, and the ignorance and unbelief incurred by the fall. Fallen as we are, we feel more pride in our national great men, than dejection at our national misfortunes from the hopefulness of our nature. Much more then, in the great kingdom and people of God;—the Saints are ever in our sight, and not as mere ineffectual ghosts or dim memories, but as if present bodily in their past selves. It is said of them, "Their works do follow them;" what they were here, such are they in heaven and in the Church. As we call them by their earthly names, so we contemplate them in their earthly characters and histories. Their acts, callings, and relations below, are types and anticipations of their present mission above. Even in the case of our Lord Himself, whose native home is the eternal heavens, it is said of Him in His state of glory, that He is "a Priest forever;" and when He comes again, He will be recognized by those who pierced Him, as being the very same that He was on earth. The only question is, whether the Blessed Virgin had a part, a real part, in the economy of grace, whether, when she was on earth, she secured by her deeds any claim on our memories? If she did, it is impossible we should put her away from us, merely because she is gone hence, and should not look at her still according to the measure of her earthly history, with gratitude and expectation. If, as St. Irenæus says, she acted the part of an Advocate, a friend in need, even in her mortal life, if as St. Jerome and St. Ambrose say, she was on

earth the great pattern of Virgins, if she had a meritorious share in bringing about our redemption, if her maternity was gained by her faith and obedience, if her Divine
Son was subject to her, and if she stood by the Cross with
a mother's heart and drank in to the full those sufferings
which it was her portion to gaze upon, it is impossible that
we should not associate these characteristics of her life on
earth with her present state of blessedness; and this surely
she anticipated, when she said in her hymn that all "generations should call her blessed."

—Letter to Dr. Pusey

OUR LADY IN SCRIPTURE

The popular astonishment, excited by our belief in the blessed Virgin's present dignity, arises from the circumstance that the bulk of men, engaged in matters of this world, have never calmly considered her historical position in the gospels, so as rightly to realize what that position imports. I do not claim for the generality of Catholics any greater powers of reflection upon the objects of their faith, than Protestants commonly have; but, putting the run of Catholics aside, there is a sufficient number of religious men among us who, instead of expending their devotional energies (as so many serious Protestants do) on abstract doctrines, such as justification by faith only, or the sufficiency of Holy Scripture, employ themselves in the contemplation of Scripture facts, and bring out before their minds in a tangible form the doctrines involved in them, and give such a substance and color to the sacred history, as to influence their brethren; and their brethren, though superficial themselves, are drawn by their Catholic instinct to accept conclusions which they could not indeed themselves have elicited, but which, when elicited, they feel to be true. However, it would be out of place to pursue this course of reasoning here; and instead of doing so, I shall take what perhaps some may think a very bold step,—I shall find the doctrine of our Lady's present exaltation in Scripture.

I mean to find it in the vision of the Woman and Child in the twelfth chapter of the Apocalypse. Now, here two objections will be made to me at once; first that such an interpretation is but poorly supported by the Fathers, and secondly that in ascribing such a picture of the Madonna (as it may be called) to the Apostolic age, I am committing an anachronism.

As to the former of these objections, I answer as follows: Christians have never gone to Scripture for proof of their doctrines, until there was actual need from the pressure of controversy. If in those times the Blessed Virgin's dignity was unchallenged on all sides, as a matter of doctrine, Scripture, as far as its argumentative matter was concerned, was likely to remain a sealed book to them. Many texts there are, which ought to find a place in ancient controversies, and the omission of which by the Fathers affords matter for more surprise; those for instance, which are real proofs of our Lord's divinity, and yet are passed over by Catholic disputants; for these bear upon a then existing controversy of the highest importance, and of the most urgent exigency.

—Letter to Dr. Pusey

ANTIQUITY OF THE MADONNA

As to the question of anachronism in interpreting the Madonna in the Virgin of the Apocalypse, so far from allowing it, I consider that it is built upon a mere imaginary fact, and that the truth of the matter lies in the very contrary direction. The Virgin and Child is *not* a mere modern idea; on the contrary, it is represented again and again, as every visitor to Rome is aware, in the paintings of the Catacombs. Mary is there drawn with the Divine Infant in her lap, she with hands extended in prayer, He with His hand in the attitude of blessing. No representation can more forcibly convey the doctrine of the high dignity of the Mother, and, I will add, of her influence with her Son. Why should the memory of His time of subjection be so dear to Christians, and so carefully preserved? The only question to be determined, is the precise date of these remarkable monuments of the first age of Christianity. That they belong to the centuries of what Anglicans call the "undivided Church" is certain; but lately investigations have been pursued, which place some of them at an earlier date than anyone anticipated as possible.

In the Catacombs we have various representations of the Virgin and Child; the latest of these belong to the early part of the fourth century, but the earliest may be from the very age of the Apostles. This conclusion is reached from the style and the skill of its composition, and from the history, locality, and existing inscriptions of the subterranean in which it is found. However we do not go so far as to insist upon so early a date; yet the utmost concession could be to refer the painting to the era of the first Antonine Emperors, that is, to a date within half a century of the death of St. John. I consider then, that, as you would use in controversy with Protestants, and fairly, the traditional doctrine of the Church in early times, as an explanation of a particular passage of Scripture, or at least as a suggestion, or as a defense, of the sense which you may wish to put upon it, quite apart from the question whether your interpretation itself is directly traditional, so it is lawful for me, though I have not the positive words of the Fathers on my side, to shelter my own interpretation of the Apostle's vision in the Apocalypse under the fact of the extant pictures of Mother and Child in the Roman Catacombs.

Again, there is another principle of Scripture interpretation which we should hold as well as Protestants, viz., when we speak of a doctrine being contained in Scripture, we do not necessarily mean that it is contained there in direct categorical terms, but that there is no satisfactory way of accounting for the language and expressions of the sacred writer s, concerning the subject-matter in question, except to suppose that they held concerning it the opinion which we hold,—that they would not have spoken as they have spoken, *unless* they held it. For myself I have ever felt the truth of this principle, as regards the Scripture proof of the Holy Trinity; I should not have found out that doctrine in the sacred text without previous traditional teaching; but, when once it is suggested from without, it commends itself as the one true interpretation, from its appositeness,—because no other view of doctrine, which can be ascribed to the inspired writers, so happily solves the obscurities and seeming inconsistencies of their teaching.

–Letter to Dr. Pusey

HOUSE OF GOLD

Why is she called a *House*? And why is she called *Golden*? Gold is the most beautiful, the most valuable, of all metals. Silver, copper, and steel may in their way be made good to the eye, but nothing is so rich, so splendid, as gold. We have few opportunities of seeing it in any quantity; but anyone who has seen a large number of bright gold coins knows how magnificent is the look of gold. Hence it is that in Scripture the Holy City is, by a figure of speech, called Golden. "The City," says St. John, "was pure gold, as it were transparent glass." He means of course to give us a notion of the wondrous beautifulness of heaven, by comparing it with what is the most beautiful of all the substances which we see on earth.

Therefore it is that Mary too is called *golden*; because her graces, her virtues, her innocence, her purity, are of that transcendent brilliancy and dazzling perfection, so costly, so exquisite, that the angels cannot, so to say, keep their eyes off her any more than *we* could help gazing upon any great work of gold.

But observe further, she is a *golden house*, or, I will rather say, a *golden palace*. Let us imagine we saw a whole palace or large church all made of gold, from the foundations to the roof; such, in regard to the number, the variety, the extent of her spiritual excellences, is Mary.

But why called a *house* or palace? And *whose* palace? She is the house and the palace of the Great King, of God Himself. Our Lord, the Coequal Son of God, once dwelt in her. He was her Guest; nay, more than a guest, for a guest comes into a house as well as leaves it. But our Lord was actually *born in* this holy house. He took His flesh and His blood from this house, from the flesh, from the veins of Mary. Rightly then was she made to be of pure gold, because she was to give of that gold to form the body of the Son of God. She was *golden* in her conception, *golden* in her birth. She went through the fire of her suffering like gold in the furnace, and when she ascended on high, she was, in the words of our hymn,

> Above all the Angels in glory untold, Standing
> next to the King in a vesture of gold.

—Meditations on the Litany of Loretto
for the Month of May

SHE STRETCHED OUT HER BRANCHES LIKE A FAIR TREE

You will find, that, in this respect, as in Mary's prerogatives themselves, there is the same careful reference to the glory of Him who gave them to her. You know, when first He went out to preach, she kept apart from Him; she interfered not with His work; and, even when He was gone up on high, yet she, a woman, went not out to preach or teach, she did not seat herself in the Apostolic chair, nor did she take any part in the priest's office. She did but humbly seek her Son in the daily Mass of those, who, though her ministers in heaven, were her superiors in the Church on earth. When she and they had left this lower scene, and she was a Queen upon her Son's right hand, not even then did she ask of Him to publish her name to the ends of the world, or to hold her up to the world's gaze, but she remained waiting for the time, when her own glory should be necessary for His.

He indeed had been from the very first proclaimed by Holy Church, and enthroned in His temple, for He was God. Ill had it served the living Oracle of Truth to have withheld from the faithful the very object of their adoration; but it was otherwise with Mary. It became her, as a creature, a mother, and a woman, to stand aside and make way for the Creator, to minister to her Son, and to win her way into the world's homage by sweet and gracious persuasion. So, when His name was dishonored, then it was that she did Him service; when Emmanuel was denied, then the Mother of God (as it were) came forward; when heretics said that God was not incarnate, then was the time for her own honors. And then, when as much as this had been accomplished, she had done with strife; she fought not for herself.

No fierce controversy, no persecuted confessors, no heresiarch, no anathema, were necessary for her gradual manifestation. As she had increased day by day in grace and merit at Nazareth, while the world knew not of her, so has she raised herself aloft silently, and has grown into her place in the Church by a tranquil influence and a natural process. She was as some fair tree, stretching forth her fruitful branches and her fragrant leaves, and overshadowing the territory of the saints. And thus, the Antiphon speaks of her: "Let thy dwelling be in Jacob, and thine inheritance in Israel, and *strike thy roots* in My elect".

Again, "And so in Sion was I established, and in the holy city I likewise rested, and in Jerusalem was my power. And I *took root* in an honorable people, and in the glorious company of the saints was I *detained*. I was exalted like a cedar in Lebanon, and as a cypress in Mount Sion; I have stretched out my branches as the terebinth, and my branches are of honor and grace." Thus was she reared without hands, and gained a modest victory, and exerts a gentle sway, which she has not claimed. When dispute arose about her among her children, she hushed it; when objections were urged against her, she waived her claims and waited, until now, in this very day, should God so will, she will win at length her most radiant crown, and, without opposing voice, and amid the jubilation of the whole Church, she will be hailed as immaculate in her conception.

—Discourses to Mixed Congregations

SANCTITY
OF MARY

THE FIRST MIRACLE OF HIS GRACE

However, a remedy had been determined in heaven; a Redeemer was at hand; God was about to do a great work, and He purposed to do it suitably; "where sin abounded, grace was to abound more". Kings of the earth, when they have sons born to them, forthwith scatter some large bounty, or raise some high memorial. They honor the day, or the place, or the heralds of the auspicious event, with some corresponding mark of favor; nor did the coming of Emmanuel innovate on the world's established custom. It was a season of grace and prodigy, and these were to be exhibited in a special manner in the person of His Mother. The course of ages was to be reversed— the tradition of evil was to be broken. A gate of light was to be opened amid the darkness, for the coming of the Just—a Virgin conceived and bore Him.

It was fitting, for His honor and glory, that she, who was the instrument of His bodily presence, should first be a miracle of His grace; it was fitting that she should triumph, where Eve had failed, and should "bruise the serpent's head" by the spotlessness of her sanctity. In some respects, indeed, the curse was not reversed. Mary came into a fallen world, and resigned herself to its laws; she, as also the Son she bore, was exposed to pain of soul and body, she was subjected to death—but she was not put under the power of sin. As grace was infused into Adam from the first moment of his creation, so that he never had experience of his natural poverty (until sin reduced him to it), so was grace given from the first in still ampler measure to Mary, and she never incurred, in fact, Adam's deprivation. She began where others end, whether in knowledge or in love. She was from the first clothed in sanctity, destined for perseverance, luminous and glorious in God's sight, and incessantly employed in meritorious acts, which continued until her last breath. Hers was emphatically "the path of the just, which, as the shining light, goes forward and increases even to the perfect day"; and sinlessness in thought, word, and deed, in small things as well as great, in venial matters as well as grievous, is surely but the natural and obvious sequel of such a beginning. If Adam might have kept himself from sin in his first state, much more shall we expect immaculate perfection in Mary.

—Discourses to Mixed Congregations

ALL WOMEN HAVE BEEN RESTORED THROUGH THE DIGNITY OF MARY

Now let us consider in what respects the Virgin Mary is Blessed; a title first given her by the Angel, and next by the Church in all ages since to this day.

I observe, that in her the curse pronounced on Eve was changed to a blessing. Eve was doomed to bear children in sorrow, but now this very dispensation, in which the token of Divine anger was conveyed, was made the means by which salvation came into the world. Christ might have descended from heaven, as He went back, and as He will come again. He might have taken on Himself a body from the ground, as Adam was given, or been formed, like Eve, in some other divinely-devised way. But, far from this, God sent forth His Son, "made of a woman." For it has been His gracious purpose to turn *all* that is ours from evil to good. Had He so pleased, He might have found, when we sinned, other beings to do Him service, casting us into hell; but He purposed to save and to change *us*. And in like manner all that belongs to us, our reason, our affections, our pursuits, our relations in life, He needs nothing put aside in His disciples, but all sanctified. Therefore, instead of sending His Son from heaven, He sent Him forth as the Son of Mary, to show that all our sorrow and all our corruption can be blessed and changed by Him. The very punishment of the fall, the very taint of original sin, admits of a cure by the coming of Christ.

But there is another portion of the original punishment

of woman, which may be considered as repealed when Christ came. It was said to the woman, "Thy husband shall rule over thee;" a sentence which has been strikingly fulfilled. Man has strength to conquer the thorns and thistles which the earth is cursed with, but the same strength has ever proved the fulfilment of the punishment awarded to the woman.

But when Christ came as the seed of the woman, He vindicated the rights and honor of His mother. Not that the distinction of ranks is destroyed under the Gospel; the woman is still made inferior to man, as he to Christ—but the slavery is done away with. St. Peter bids the husband "give honor unto the wife, *because* the weaker, in that both are heirs of the grace of life." (1 Pet. 3:7). And St. Paul, while enjoining subjection upon her, speaks of the especial blessedness promised to her in being the appointed entrance of the Savior into the world. "Adam was first formed, then Eve; and Adam was not deceived, but the woman being deceived was in the transgression." But "notwithstanding, she shall be saved through the Child-bearing;" (1 Tim. 2:15), that is, through the birth of Christ from Mary, which was a blessing, as upon all mankind, so peculiarly upon the woman. Accordingly, from that time, Marriage has not only been restored to its original dignity, but even gifted with a spiritual privilege, as the outward symbol of the heavenly union subsisting betwixt Christ and His Church.

In this way, the Blessed Virgin, in bearing our Lord, has taken off or lightened the peculiar disgrace which the woman inherited for seducing Adam, sanctifying the one part of it, repealing the other.

But further, she is doubtless to be accounted blessed and favored in herself, as well as in the benefits she has done us. Who can estimate the holiness and perfection of her, who was chosen to be the Mother of Christ? If to him that has, more is to be given, and holiness and Divine favor go together, then what must have been the transcendent purity of her, whom the Creator Spirit condescended to overshadow with His miraculous presence?

—Parochial and Plain Sermons, II

HOLY MARY

God alone can claim the attribute of holiness. Hence we say in the Hymn, "*Tu solus sanctus*," "You alone are holy." By holiness we mean the absence of whatever sullies, dims, and degrades a rational nature; all that is most opposite and contrary to sin and guilt.

We say that God alone is *holy*, though in truth *all* His high attributes are possessed by Him in that fulness, that it may be truly said that He alone has them. Thus, as to goodness, our Lord said to the young man, "None is good but God alone." He too alone is Power, He alone is Wisdom, He alone is Providence, Love, Mercy, Justice, Truth. This is true; but holiness is singled out as His special prerogative, because it marks more than His other attributes, not only His superiority over all His creatures, but emphatically His separation from them. Hence, we read in the Book of Job, "Can man be justified compared with God, or he that is born of a woman appear clean? Behold, even the moon doth not shine, and the stars are not pure, in His sight." "Behold, among His saints none is unchangeable, and the Heavens are not pure in His sight."

This we must receive and understand in the first place; but secondly, we know too, that, in His mercy, He has communicated in various measures His great attributes to His rational creatures, and, first of all, as being most necessary, holiness. Thus Adam, from the time of his creation, was gifted, over and above his nature as man, with the grace of God, to unite him to God, and to make him holy.

Grace is therefore called holy grace; and, as being holy, it is the connecting principle between God and man. Adam in Paradise might have had knowledge, and skill, and many virtues; but these gifts did not unite him to his Creator. It was holiness that united him, for it is said by St. Paul, "Without holiness no man shall see God."

And so again, when man fell and lost *this* holy grace, he had various gifts still adhering to him; he might be, in a certain measure, true, merciful, loving, and just; but these virtues did not unite him to God. What he needed was holiness; and therefore, the first act of God's goodness to us in the Gospel is to take us out of our *unholy* state by means of the sacrament of Baptism, and by the grace then given us to re-open the communications, so long closed, between the soul and heaven.

We see then the force of our Lady's title, when we call her "*Holy* Mary." When God would prepare a human mother for His Son, this was why He began by giving her an immaculate conception. He began, not by giving her the gift of love, or truthfulness, or gentleness, or devotion, though according to the occasion she had them all. But He began His great work before she was born; before she could think, speak, or act, by making her *holy*, and thereby, while on earth, a citizen of heaven. "*Tota* pulchra es, Maria!" Nothing of the deformity of sin was ever hers. Thus, she differs from all saints. There have been great missionaries, confessors, bishops, doctors, pastors. They have done great works, and have taken with them numberless converts or penitents to heaven. They have suffered much, and have a superabundance of merits to show. But Mary in this way resembles her Divine Son, viz., that, as He, being God, is separate by holiness from all creatures, so she is separate from all Saints and Angels, as being "*full of grace.*"

—*Meditations on the Litany of Loretto
for the Month of May*

VIRGO VENERANDA

We use the word "*Venerable*" generally of what is *old*. That is because only what is old has commonly those qualities which excite reverence or veneration.

It is a great history, a great character, a maturity of virtue, goodness, experience, that excite our reverence, and these commonly cannot belong to the young.

But this is not true when we are considering Saints. A short life with them is a long one. Thus, Holy Scripture says, "Venerable age is not that of long time, nor counted by the number of years, but it is the *understanding* of a man that is gray hairs, and a spotless life is old age. The just man, if he be cut short by death, shall be at rest; being made perfect in a short time, he fulfilled a long time."

Nay, there is a heathen writer, who knew nothing of Saints, who lays it down that even to children, to all children, a great reverence should be paid, and that on the ground of their being as yet innocent. And this is a feeling very widely felt and expressed in all countries; so much so that the sight of those who have not sinned (that is, who are not yet old enough to have fallen into mortal sin) has, on the very score of that innocent, smiling youthfulness, often disturbed and turned the plunderer or the assassin in the midst of his guilty doings, filled him with a sudden fear, and brought him, if not to repentance, at least to change of purpose.

And, to pass from the thought of the lowest to the Highest, what shall we say of the Eternal God (if we may safely speak of Him at all) but that He, *because* He is eternal, is ever *young*, without a beginning, and therefore without change, and, in the fulness and perfection of His incomprehensible attributes, now just what He was a million years ago? He is truly called in Scripture the "Ancient of Days," and is therefore infinitely venerable; yet He needs not old age to make him venerable; He has really nothing of those human attendants on venerableness which the sacred writers are obliged figuratively to ascribe to Him, in order to make us feel that profound abasement and reverential awe which we ought to entertain at the thought of Him.

And so of the great Mother of God, as far as a creature can be like the Creator; her ineffable purity and utter freedom from any shadow of sin, her Immaculate Conception, her ever-virginity—these her prerogatives (in spite of her extreme youth at the time when Gabriel came to her) are such as to lead us to exclaim in the prophetic words of Scripture both with awe and with exultation, "Thou art the glory of Jerusalem and the joy of Israel; thou art the honor of our people; therefore hath the hand of the Lord strengthened thee, and therefore art thou blessed forever."

—*Meditations on the Litany of Loretto*
for the Month of May

CO-REDEMPTRIX

I shall dwell for a while upon two inferences, which it is obvious to draw from the rudimental doctrine itself. The first relates to the sanctity of the Blessed Virgin, the second to her dignity.

Her sanctity. She holds, as the Fathers teach us, that office in our restoration which Eve held in our fall:—now, in the first place, what were Eve's endowments to enable her to enter upon her trial? She could not have stood against the wiles of the devil, though she was innocent and sinless, without the grant of a large grace. And this she had—a heavenly gift, which was over and above and additional to that nature of hers, which she received from Adam, a gift which had been given to Adam also before her, at the very time (as it is commonly held) of his original formation. This is Anglican doctrine, as well as Catholic; it is the doctrine of Bishop Bull. He has written a dissertation on the point. He speaks of the doctrine which "many of the Schoolmen affirm, that Adam was created in grace, that is, received a principle of grace and divine life from his very creation, or in the moment of the infusion of his soul; of which," he says, "for my own part I have little doubt." Again, he says, "It is abundantly manifest from the many testimonies alleged, that the ancient doctors of the Church did, with a general consent, acknowledge, that our first parents in the state of integrity, had in them something more than nature, that is, were endowed with the divine principle of the Spirit, in order to a supernatural felicity."

Now, taking this for granted, because I know that some maintain it as well as we do, I ask: Have you any intention to deny that Mary was as fully endowed as Eve? is it any violent inference, that she, who was to co-operate in the redemption of the world, at least was not less endowed with power from on high, than she who, given as a help-mate to her husband, did in the event but cooperate with him for its ruin? If Eve was raised above human nature by that indwelling moral gift which we call grace, is it rash to say that Mary had even a greater grace? And this consideration gives significance to the Angel's salutation of her as "full of grace,"—an interpretation of the original word which is undoubtedly the right one, as soon as we resist the common Protestant assumption that grace is a mere external approbation or acceptance, answering to the word "favor," whereas it is, as the Fathers teach, a real inward condition or superadded quality of soul. And if Eve had this supernatural inward gift given her from the first moment of her personal existence, is it possible to deny that Mary too had this gift from the very first moment of her personal existence? I do not know how to resist this inference—well, this is simply and literally the doctrine of the Immaculate Conception. I say the doctrine of the Immaculate Conception is in its substance this, and nothing more or less than this (putting aside the question of degrees of grace); and it really does seem to me bound up in the doctrine of the Fathers, that Mary is the second Eve.

—Letter to Dr. Pusey

THE
IMMACULATE
CONCEPTION

CONCEIVED WITHOUT
ORIGINAL SIN

It is indeed to me a most strange phenomenon that so many learned and devout men stumble at this doctrine. I can only account for it by supposing that in matter of fact they do not know what we mean by the Immaculate Conception; and reading that I have done has borne out my suspicion.

I do not see how anyone who holds the Catholic doctrine of the supernatural endowments of our first parents has fair reason for doubting our doctrine about the Blessed Virgin. It has no reference whatever to her parents, but simply to her own person. It does but affirm that, together with the nature which she inherited from her parents, that is, her own nature, she had a superadded fulness of grace, and that from the first moment of her existence. Suppose Eve had stood the trial, and not lost her first grace; and suppose she had eventually had children, those children from the first moment of their existence would, through divine bounty, have received the same privilege that she had ever had; that is, as she was taken from Adam's side, in a garment, so to say, of grace, so they in turn would have received what may be called an immaculate conception. They would have then been conceived in grace, as in fact they are conceived in sin. What is there difficult in this doctrine? What is there unnatural? Mary may be called, as it were, a daughter of Eve unfallen.

But it may be said: How does this enable us to say that she was conceived without *original sin*? If Anglicans knew what we mean by original sin, they would not ask the question. Our doctrine of original sin is not the same as the Protestant doctrine. "Original sin," with us, cannot be called sin, in the mere ordinary sense of the word "sin." It is a term denoting Adam's sin as transferred to us, or the state to which Adam's sin reduces his children; but by Protestants it seems to be understood as sin, in much the same sense as actual sin. We, with the Fathers, think of it as something negative, Protestants as something positive. Protestants hold that it is a disease, a radical change of nature, an active poison internally corrupting the soul, infecting its primary elements, and disorganizing it; and they fancy that we ascribe a different nature from ours to the Blessed Virgin, different from that of her parents, and from that of fallen Adam.

We hold nothing of the kind; we consider that in Adam she died, as others; that she was included, together with the whole race, in Adam's sentence. Moreover, she incurred his debt, as we do, but for the sake of Him who was to redeem her and us upon the Cross, to her the debt was remitted by anticipation, on her the sentence was not carried out, except indeed as regards her natural death, for she died when her time came, as others. All this we teach, but we deny that she had original sin, seeing that by original sin we mean, as I have already said, something negative, viz., this only, the *deprivation* of that supernatural unmerited grace which Adam and Eve had on their first formation. Mary could not merit, any more than they, the restoration of that grace; but it was restored to her by God's free bounty, from the very first moment of her existence, and thereby, in fact, she never came under the original curse, which consisted in the loss of it. And she had this special privilege, in order to fit her to become the Mother of her and our Redeemer, to fit her mentally, spiritually for it; so that, by the aid of the first grace, she might so grow in grace, that, when the Angel came and her Lord was at hand, she might be "full of grace," prepared as far as a creature could be prepared, to receive Him into her bosom.

—Letter to Dr. Pusey

TWO LADDERS

As to primitive notion about our Blessed Lady, really, the frequent contrast of Mary with Eve seems very strong indeed. It is found in St. Justin, St. Irenaeus, and Tertullian, three of the earliest Fathers, and in three distinct continents—Gaul, Africa, and Syria. For instance, "the knot formed by Eve's disobedience was untied by the obedience of Mary; that what the Virgin Eve tied through unbelief, that the Virgin Mary unties through faith." Again, "The Virgin Mary becomes the Advocate (Paraclete) of the Virgin Eve, that *as* mankind has been bound to death *through* a Virgin, *through* a Virgin it may be saved, the balance being preserved, a Virgin's disobedience by a Virgin's obedience" (St. Irenaeus, *Haer.* v. 19). Again, "As Eve, becoming disobedient, became *the cause* of death to herself and *to all mankind, so* Mary, too, bearing the predestined Man, and yet a Virgin, being obedient, became the cause of Salvation both to herself and to all mankind." Again, "Eve being a Virgin, and incorrupt, bore disobedience and death, but Mary the Virgin, receiving faith and joy, when Gabriel the Angel evangelized her, answered, 'Be it unto me,'" &c. Again, "What Eve failed in believing, Mary by believing *hath* blotted out."

Now, can we refuse to see that, according to these Fathers, who are earliest of the early, Mary was a *typical woman* like Eve, that both were endued with special gifts of grace, and that Mary succeeded where Eve failed?

Moreover, what light they cast upon St. Alphonsus's

doctrine, of which a talk is sometimes made, of the two ladders. You see according to these most early Fathers, Mary *undoes* what Eve had done; mankind is *saved through* a Virgin; the *obedience* of Mary becomes the *cause of salvation to all mankind*. Moreover, the distinct way in which Mary does this is pointed out when she is called by the early Fathers an *Advocate*. The word is used of our Lord and the Holy Spirit—of our Lord; as interceding for us in His own Person; of the Holy Spirit, as interceding in the Saints. This is the *white* way, as our Lord's own special way is the *red* way, viz. of atoning Sacrifice.

Further still; what light these passages cast on two texts of Scripture. *Our* reading is, "*She* shall bruise thy head." Now, this fact alone of our reading, "She shall bruise," has some weight, for *why* should not, perhaps, our reading be the right one? But take the comparison of Scripture with Scripture, and see how the whole hangs together as we interpret it. A war between a woman and the serpent is spoken of in Genesis. *Who* is the serpent? Scripture nowhere says till the twelfth chapter of the Apocalypse. There at last, for the first time, the "Serpent" is interpreted to mean the Evil Spirit. Now, *how* is he introduced? Why, by the vision *again* of a Woman, his enemy—and just as, in the first vision in Genesis, the Woman has a "seed," so here a "Child." Can we help saying, then; that the Woman is Mary in the third of Genesis? And if so, and our reading is right, the first prophecy ever given contrasts the Second Woman with the First—Mary with Eve, just as St. Justin, St. Irenaeus, and Tertullian do.

Moreover, see the direct bearing of this upon the Immaculate Conception. There was *war* between the woman and the Serpent. This is most emphatically fulfilled if she had nothing to do with sin—for, so far as anyone sins, he has an alliance with the Evil One.

—*Memorandum on the Immaculate Conception*

MOST PURE VIRGIN

By the Immaculate Conception of the Blessed Virgin is meant the great revealed truth that she was conceived in the womb of her mother, St. Anne, without original sin.

Since the fall of Adam all mankind, his descendants, are conceived and born in sin. "Behold," says the inspired writer in the Psalm *Miserere*—"Behold, I was conceived in iniquity, and in sin did my mother conceive me." That sin which belongs to every one of us, and is ours from the first moment of our existence, is the sin of unbelief and disobedience, by which Adam lost Paradise. We, as the children of Adam, are heirs to the consequences of his sin, and have forfeited in him that spiritual robe of grace and holiness which he had given him by his Creator at the time that he was made. In this state of forfeiture and disinheritance we are all of us conceived and born; and the ordinary way by which we are taken out of it is the Sacrament of Baptism.

But Mary *never* was in this state; she was by the eternal decree of God exempted from it. From eternity, God, the Father, Son, and Holy Spirit, decreed to create the race of man, and, foreseeing the fall of Adam, decreed to redeem the whole race by the Son's taking flesh and suffering on the Cross. In that same incomprehensible, eternal instant, in which the Son of God was born of the Father, was also the decree passed of man's redemption through Him. He who was born from Eternity was born by an eternal decree to save us in Time, and to redeem the whole race; and Mary's redemption was determined in that special manner which we call the Immaculate Conception. It was decreed, not that she should be *cleansed* from sin, but that she should, from the first moment of her being, be *preserved* from sin; so that the Evil One never had any part in her. Therefore, she was a child of Adam and Eve as if they had never fallen; she did not share with them their sin; she inherited the gifts and graces (and more than those) which Adam and Eve possessed in Paradise. This is her prerogative, and the foundation of all those salutary truths which are revealed to us concerning her. Let us say then with all holy souls, *Virgin most pure, conceived without original sin, Mary, pray for us.*

—Meditations on the Litany of Loretto
for the Month of May

THE VIRGIN PROCLAIMED

Mary is the *Virgo Praedicanda*, that is, the Virgin who is to be proclaimed, to be heralded, literally, to be *preached*.

We are accustomed to preach abroad that which is wonderful, strange, rare, novel, important. Thus, when our Lord was coming, St. John the Baptist *preached* Him; then, the Apostles went into the wide world, and *preached* Christ. What is the highest, the rarest, the choicest prerogative of Mary? It is that she was without sin. When a woman in the crowd cried out to our Lord, "Blessed is the womb that bare Thee!" He answered, "More blessed are they who hear the word of God and keep it." Those words were fulfilled in Mary. She was filled with grace *in order* to be the Mother of God. But it was a higher gift than her maternity to be thus sanctified and thus pure. Our Lord indeed would not have become her son *unless* He had first sanctified her; but still, the greater blessedness was to have that perfect sanctification. *This* then is why she is the *Virgo Praedicanda*; she is deserving to be preached abroad because she never committed any sin, even the least; because sin had no part in her; because, through the fulness of God's grace, she never thought a thought, or spoke a word, or did an action, which was displeasing, which was not most pleasing, to Almighty God; because in her was displayed the greatest triumph over the enemy of souls. Wherefore, when all seemed lost, in order to show what He could do for us all by dying for us; in order to show what human nature, His work, was capable of becoming; to show how utterly He could bring to naught the utmost efforts, the most concentrated malice of the foe, and reverse all the consequences of the Fall, our Lord began, even before His coming, to do His most wonderful act of redemption, in the person of her who was to be His Mother. By the merit of that Blood which was to be shed, He interposed to hinder her incurring the sin of Adam, before He had made on the Cross atonement for it. And therefore, it is that we *preach* her who is the subject of this wonderful grace.

But she was the *Virgo Praedicanda* for another reason. When, why, what things do we preach? We preach what is not known, that it may *become* known. And hence the Apostles are said in Scripture to "preach Christ." To whom? To those who knew Him not—to the heathen world. Not to those who knew Him, but to those who did not know Him. Preaching is a gradual work: first one lesson, then another. Thus, were the heathen brought into the Church *gradually*. And in like manner, the preaching of Mary to the children of the Church, and the devotion paid to her by them, has *grown*, grown gradually, with successive ages. Not so much preached about her in *early* times as in *later*. First, she was preached as the Virgin of Virgins—then as the Mother of God—then as glorious in her Assumption— then as the Advocate of sinners—then as Immaculate in her Conception. And this last has been the special preaching of the present century; and thus, that which was earliest in her own history is the latest in the Church's recognition of her.

—Meditations on the Litany of Loretto
for the Month of May

THE
ASSUMPTION

LEAVING THE WORLD

Miracles must be wrought for some great end; and if the course of things fell back again into a natural order before its termination, how could we but feel a disappointment? If we were told that this certainly was to be, how could we but judge the information improbable and difficult to believe? Now this applies to the history of our Lady. I say, it would be a greater miracle if, her life being what it was, her death was like that of other men, than if it were such as to correspond to her life. Who can conceive, my brethren, that God should so repay the debt, which He condescended to owe to His Mother, for the elements of His human body, as to allow the flesh and blood from which it was taken to rot in the grave? Do the sons of men thus deal with their mothers? do they not nourish and sustain them in their feebleness, and keep them in life while they are able? Or who can conceive that that virginal frame, which never sinned, was to undergo the death of a sinner? Why should she share the curse of Adam, who had no share in his fall? "Dust thou art, and into dust thou shalt return," was the sentence upon sin; she then, who was not a sinner, fitly never saw corruption. She died, then, as we hold, because even our Lord and Savior died; she died, as she suffered, because she was in this world, because she was in a state of things in which suffering and death are the rule.

She lived under their external sway; and, as she obeyed Caesar by coming for enrolment to Bethlehem, so did she, when God willed it, yield to the tyranny of death, and was dissolved into soul and body, as well as others. But though she died as well as others, she died not as others die; for, through the merits of her Son, by whom she was what she was, by the grace of Christ which in her had antici- pated sin, which had filled her with light, which had puri- fied her flesh from all defilement, she was also saved from disease and malady, and all that weakens and decays the bodily frame.

And therefore, she died in private. It became Him, who died for the world, to die in the world's sight; it became the Great Sacrifice to be lifted up on high, as a light that could not be hid. But she, the lily of Eden, who had always dwelt out of the sight of man, fittingly did she die in the garden's shade, and amid the sweet flowers in which she had lived. Her departure made no noise in the world. The Church went about her common duties, preaching, converting, suffering; there were persecutions, there was fleeing from place to place, there were mar- tyrs, there were triumphs; at length the rumor spread abroad that the Mother of God was no longer upon earth. Pilgrims went to and fro; they sought for her relics, but they found them not; did she die at Ephesus? or did she die at Jerusalem? reports varied; but her tomb could not be pointed out, or if it was found, it was open; and instead of her pure and fragrant body, there was a growth of lilies from the earth which she had touched.

So, inquirers went home marveling, and waiting for further light. And then it was said, how that when her dissolution was at hand, and her soul was to pass in triumph before the judgment-seat of her Son, the apostles were suddenly gathered together in the place, even in the Holy City, to bear part in the joyful ceremonial; how that they buried her with fitting rites; how that the third day, when they came to the tomb, they found it empty, and angelic choirs with their glad voices were heard singing day and night the glories of their risen Queen. But, however we feel towards the details of this history (nor is there anything in it which will be unwelcome or difficult to piety), so much cannot be doubted, from the consent of the whole Catholic world and the revelations made to holy souls, that, as is befitting, she is, soul and body, with her Son and God in heaven, and that we are enabled to celebrate, not only her death, but her Assumption.

—*Discourses to Mixed Congregations*

IMITATION OF MARY

Now, my dear brethren, what is befitting in us, if all that I have been telling you is befitting in Mary? What is befitting in the children of such a Mother, but an imitation of her devotion, her meekness, her simplicity, her modesty, and her sweetness, if the Mother of Emmanuel ought to be the first of creatures in sanctity and in beauty? Or, if it became her to be free from all sin from the very first, and from the moment she received her first grace to begin to merit more? Or, if such as was her beginning, such was her end, her conception immaculate and her death an assumption? If she died, but revived, and is exalted on high? Her glories are not only for the sake of her Son, they are for our sakes also. Let us copy her faith, who received God's message by the angel without a doubt; her patience, who endured St. Joseph's surprise without a word; her obedience, who went up to Bethlehem in the winter and bore our Lord in a stable; her meditative spirit, who pondered in her heart what she saw and heard about Him; her fortitude, whose heart the sword went through; her self-surrender, who gave Him up during His ministry and consented to His death.

Above all, let us imitate her purity, who, rather than relinquish her virginity, was willing to lose Him for a Son. O my dear children, young men and young women, what need have you of the intercession of the Virgin-mother, of her help, of her pattern, in this respect! What shall bring you forward in the narrow way, if you live in the world, but the thought and patronage of Mary? What shall seal your senses, what shall tranquillize your heart, when sights and sounds of danger are around you, but Mary? What shall give you patience and endurance, when you are wearied out with the length of the conflict with evil, with the unceasing necessity of precautions, with the irksomeness of observing them, with the tediousness of their repetition, with the strain upon your mind, with your forlorn and cheerless condition, but a loving communion with her!

She will comfort you in your discouragements, solace you in your fatigues, raise you after your falls, reward you for your successes. She will show you her Son, your God and your all. When your spirit within you is excited, or relaxed, or depressed, when it loses its balance, when it is restless and wayward, when it is sick of what it has, and hankers after what it has not, when your eye is solicited with evil and your mortal frame trembles under the shadow of the tempter, what will bring you to yourselves, to peace and to health, but the cool breath of the Immaculate and the fragrance of the Rose of Sharon? It is the boast of the Catholic Religion, that it has the gift of making the young heart chaste. Why is this, but that it gives us Jesus Christ for our food, and Mary for our nursing Mother?

—Discourses to Mixed Congregations

MOST FAVORED DAUGHTER

As soon as we apprehend by faith the great fundamental truth that Mary is the Mother of God, other wonderful truths follow in its train; and one of these is that she was exempt from the ordinary lot of mortals, which is not only to die, but to become earth to earth, ashes to ashes, dust to dust. Die she must, and die she did, as her Divine Son died, for He was man; but various reasons have approved themselves to holy writers, why, although her body was for a while separated from her soul and consigned to the tomb, yet it did not remain there, but was speedily united to her soul again, and raised by our Lord to a new and eternal life of heavenly glory.

And the most obvious reason for so concluding is this—that *other* servants of God have been raised from the grave by the power of God, and it is not to be supposed that our Lord would have granted any such privilege to anyone else without also granting it to His own Mother.

We are told by St. Matthew, that after our Lord's death upon the Cross "the graves were opened, and many bodies of the saints that had slept"—that is, slept the sleep of death, "arose, and coming out of the tombs after His Resurrection, came into the Holy City, and appeared to many." St. Matthew says, "*many* bodies of the Saints"—that is, the holy Prophets, Priests, and Kings of former times—rose again in anticipation of the last day.

Can we suppose that Abraham, or David, or Isaias, or Hezekiah, should have been thus favored, and not God's own Mother? Had she not a claim on the love of her Son to have what any others had? Was she not nearer to Him than the greatest of the Saints before her? And is it conceivable that the law of the grave should admit of relaxation in their case, and not in hers? Therefore, we confidently say that our Lord, having preserved her from sin and the consequences of sin by His Passion, lost no time in pouring out the full merits of that Passion upon her body as well as her soul.

Original sin had not been found in her, by the wear of her senses, and the waste of her frame, and the decrepitude of years, propagating death. She died, but her death was a mere fact, not an effect; and, when it was over, it ceased to be. She died that she might live, she died as a matter of form or (as I may call it) an observance, in order to fulfil, what is called, the debt of nature,—not primarily for herself or because of sin, but to submit herself to her condition, to glorify God, to do what her Son did; not however as her Son and Savior, with any suffering for any special end; not with a martyr's death, for her martyrdom had been in living; not as an atonement, for man could not make it, and One had made it, and made it for all; but in order to finish her course, and to receive her crown.

—*Meditations on the Litany of Loretto*
for the Month of May

THE SINLESS MOTHER

Another consideration which has led devout minds to believe in the Assumption of our Lady into heaven after her death, without waiting for the general resurrection at the last day, is furnished by the doctrine of her Immaculate Conception.

By her Immaculate Conception is meant, that not only did she never commit any sin whatever, even venial, in thought, word, or deed, but further than this, that the guilt of Adam, or what is called original sin, never was her guilt, as it is the guilt attaching to all other descendants of Adam.

By her Assumption is meant that not only her soul, but her body also, was taken up to heaven upon her death, so that there was no long period of her sleeping in the grave, as is the case with others, even great Saints, who wait for the last day for the resurrection of their bodies.

One reason for believing in our Lady's Assumption is that her Divine Son loved her too much to let her body remain in the grave. A second reason—that now before us—is this, that she was not only dear to the Lord as a mother is dear to a son, but also that she was so transcendently holy, so full, so overflowing with grace. Adam and Eve were created upright and sinless, and had a large measure of God's grace bestowed upon them; and, in consequence, their bodies would never have crumbled into dust, had they not sinned; upon which it was said to them, "Dust thou art, and unto dust thou shalt return." If Eve, the beautiful daughter of God, never would have become dust and ashes unless she had sinned, shall we not say that Mary, having never sinned, retained the gift which Eve by sinning lost? What had Mary done to forfeit the privilege given to our first parents in the beginning? Was her comeliness to be turned into corruption, and her fine gold to become dim, without reason assigned? Impossible. Therefore, we believe that, though she died for a short hour, as did our Lord Himself, yet, like Him, and by His Almighty power, she was raised again from the grave.

She is also called the Tower of David. A tower, in its simplest idea, is a fabric for defense against enemies. David, King of Israel, built for this purpose a notable tower; and as he is a figure or type of our Lord, so is his tower a figure denoting our Lord's Virgin Mother.

She is called the *Tower* of David because she had so signally fulfilled the office of defending her Divine Son from the assaults of His foes. It is customary with those who are not Catholics to fancy that the honors we pay to her interfere with the supreme worship which we pay to Him; that in Catholic teaching she eclipses Him. But this is the very reverse of the truth.

—Meditations on the Litany of Loretto
for the Month of May

THE MORNING STAR

What is the nearest approach in the way of symbols, in this world of sight and sense, to represent to us the glories of that higher world which is beyond our bodily perceptions? What are the truest tokens and promises here, poor though they may be, of what one day we hope to see hereafter, as being beautiful and rare? Whatever they may be, surely the Blessed Mother of God may claim them as her own. And so, it is; two of them are ascribed to her as her titles, in her Litany—the stars above, and flowers below. She is at once the *Rosa Mystica* (Mystical Rose) and the *Stella Matutina* (Morning Star).

And of these two, both of them well suited to her, the Morning Star becomes her best, and that for three reasons.

First, the rose belongs to this earth, but the star is placed in high heaven. Mary now has no part in this nether world. No change, no violence from fire, water, earth, or air, affects the stars above; and they show themselves, ever bright and marvelous, in all regions of this globe, and to all the tribes of men.

And next, the rose has but a short life; its decay is as sure as it was graceful and fragrant in its noon. But Mary, like the stars, abides forever, as lustrous now as she was on the day of her Assumption; as pure and perfect, when her Son comes in judgment, as she is now.

Lastly, it is Mary's prerogative to be the *Morning* Star, which heralds in the sun. She does not shine for herself, or from herself, but she is the reflection of her and our

Redeemer, and she glorifies *Him*. When she appears in the darkness, we know that He is close at hand.

If Mary's glory is so very great, how cannot His be greater still who is the Lord and God of Mary? He is infinitely above His Mother; and all that grace which filled her is but the superfluities of His incomprehensible Sanctity. And history teaches us the same lesson. Look at the Protestant countries which threw off all devotion to her three centuries ago, under the notion that to put her from their thoughts would be exalting the praises of her Son. Has that consequence really followed from their profane conduct towards her? Just the reverse—the countries, Germany, Switzerland, England, which so acted, have in great measure ceased to worship Him, and have given up their belief in His Divinity; while the Catholic Church, wherever she is to be found, adores Christ as true God and true Man, as firmly as ever she did, and strange indeed would it be, if it ever happened otherwise.

He is Alpha and Omega, the First and the Last, the Beginning and the End. Behold He comes quickly, and His reward is with Him, to render to everyone according to his works. "Surely I come quickly. Amen. Come, Lord Jesus."

—Meditations on the Litany of Loretto
for the Month of May

INTERCESSORY
POWER OF THE
BLESSED VIRGIN

ALL GRACE COMES FROM THE HANDS OF MARY

Certain statements may be true, under circumstances and in a particular time and place, which are abstractedly false; and hence it may be very unfair in a controversialist to interpret by an English or a modern rule, whatever may have been asserted by a foreign or medieval author. To say, for instance, dogmatically, that no one can be saved without personal devotion to the Blessed Virgin, would be an untenable proposition; yet it might be true of this man or that, or of this or that country at this or that date; and, if that very statement has ever been made by any writer of consideration (and this has to be ascertained), then perhaps it was made precisely under these exceptional circumstances. If an Italian preacher made it, I should feel no disposition to doubt him, at least if he spoke of Italian youths and Italian maidens.

But now, as to the fact, by whom is it said that to pray to our Lady and the Saints is necessary to salvation? The proposition of St. Alphonsus is, that "God gives no grace except through Mary;" that is through her intercession. But intercession is one thing, devotion is another. And Suarez says, "It is the universal sentiment that the intercession of Mary is not only useful, but also in a certain manner necessary;" but still it is the question of her intercession, not of our invocation of her, not of devotion to her. If it were so, no Protestant could be saved; if it were so, there would be grave reasons for doubting of the salvation of St. Chrysostom or St. Athanasius, or of the primitive Martyrs; nay, I should like to know whether St. Augustine, in all his voluminous writings, directly invokes her once.

Our Lord died for those heathens who did not know Him, and His Mother intercedes for those Christians who do not know her, and she intercedes according to His will. When He wills to save a particular soul, she at once prays for it. I say, He wills indeed according to her prayer, but then she prays according to His will. Although, then it is natural and prudent for those to have recourse to her, who from the Church's teaching know her power, yet it cannot be said that devotion to her is a *sine-quâ-non* of salvation. Some indeed of the authors, whom you quote, go farther. They do speak of devotion, but even then, they do not enunciate the general proposition which I have been disallowing. For instance, they say, "It is morally impossible for those to be saved who *neglect* the devotion to the Blessed Virgin;" but a simple omission is one thing, and neglect another. "It is impossible for any to be saved who *turns away* from her," yes; but to "turn away" is to offer some positive disrespect or insult towards her, and that with sufficient knowledge; and I certainly think it would be a very grave act, if in a Catholic country (and of such the writers were speaking, for they knew of no other), with Ave-Marias sounding in the air, and images of the Madonna in every street and road, a Catholic broke off or gave up a practice that was universal, and in which he was brought up, and deliberately put her name out of his thoughts.

−Letter to Dr. Pusey

THE WEAPON OF THE MOTHER OF GOD IS PRAYER

Intercession is a first principle of the Church's life; next, the vital force of that intercession, as an availing power, is, (according to the will of God), sanctity. This seems to be suggested by a passage of St. Paul, in which the Supreme Intercessor is said to be the Spirit:— "the Spirit Himself makes intercession for us; He makes intercession for the saints according to God." And, indeed, the truth thus implied, is expressly brought out for us in other parts of Scripture, in the form both of doctrine and of example. The words of the man born blind speak the common-sense of nature:— "if any man be a worshiper of God, him He heareth." And Apostles confirm them:— "the prayer of a just man availeth much," and "whatever we ask, we receive, because we keep his commandments." Then, as for examples, we read of the Almighty's revealing to Abraham and Moses beforehand, His purposes of wrath, in order that by their intercessions they might avert its execution. To the friends of Job it was said, "My servant Job shall pray for you; his face I will accept." Elijah by his prayer shut and opened the heavens. Elsewhere we read of "Jeremias, Moses, and Samuel;" and of "Noah, Daniel, and Job," as being great mediators between God and His people. One instance is given us, which testifies the continuance of this high office beyond this life. Lazarus, in the parable, is seen in Abraham's bosom. It is usual to pass over this striking passage with the remark that it is a Jewish mode of speech; whereas, Jewish belief or not, it is recognized and sanctioned by our Lord Himself. What do Catholics teach about the Blessed Virgin more wonderful than this? If Abraham, not yet ascended on high, had charge of Lazarus, what offense is it to affirm the like of her, who was not merely as Abraham, "the friend," but was the very "Mother of God"?

It may be added, that, if sanctity was wanting, there could be no influence with our Lord, nor could one be one of His company. Still, as the Gospel shows, He on various occasions actually did allow those who were near Him to be the channels of introducing supplicants to Him or of gaining miracles from Him, as in the instance of the miracle of the loaves. If on one occasion, He seems to repel His Mother, when she told Him that wine was wanting for the guests at the marriage feast, it is obvious to remark on it, that, by saying that she was then separated from Him ("What have I to do with thee?") *because* His hour was not yet come, He implied, that when that hour was come, such separation would be at an end. Moreover, in fact He did at her intercession work the miracle to which her words pointed.

I consider it impossible then, for those who believe the Church to be one vast body in heaven and on earth, in which every holy creature of God has his place, and of which prayer is the life, when once they recognize the sanctity and dignity of the Blessed Virgin, not to perceive immediately, that her office above is one of perpetual intercession for the faithful militant, and that our very relation to her must be that of clients to a patron, and that, in the eternal enmity which exists between the woman and the serpent, while the serpent's strength lies in being the Tempter, the weapon of the Second Eve and Mother of God is prayer.

—Letter to Dr. Pusey

THE BOAST OF JESUS AND MARY

Such is her prerogative of sinless perfection, and it is, as her maternity, for the sake of Emmanuel; hence she answered the Angel's salutation, *Gratia plena* (full of grace), with the humble acknowledgment, *Ecce ancilla Domini*; "Behold the handmaid of the Lord". And like to this is her third prerogative, which follows both from her maternity and from her purity, and which I will mention as completing the enumeration of her glories. I mean her intercessory power. For, if "God heareth not sinners, but if a man be a worshiper of Him, and do His will, him He heareth"; if "the continual prayer of a just man availeth much"; if faithful Abraham was required to pray for Abimelech, "for he was a prophet"; if patient Job was to "pray for his friends," for he had "spoken right things before God"; if meek Moses, by lifting up his hands, turned the battle in favor of Israel against Amalec; why should we wonder at hearing that Mary, the only spotless child of Adam's seed, has a transcendent influence with the God of grace? And if the Gentiles at Jerusalem sought Philip, because he was an Apostle, when they desired access to Jesus, and Philip spoke to Andrew, as still more closely in our Lord's confidence, and then both came to Him, is it strange that the Mother should have power with the Son, distinct in kind from that of the purest angel and the most triumphant saint? If we have faith to admit the Incarnation itself, we must admit it in its fulness; why then should we start at the gracious appointments which arise out of it, or are necessary to it, or are included in it? If the Creator comes on earth in the form of a servant and a creature, why may not His Mother, on the other hand, rise to be the Queen of heaven, and be clothed with the sun, and have the moon under her feet?

It is the boast of the Catholic Religion, that it has the gift of making the young heart chaste; and why is this, but that it gives us Jesus Christ for our food, and Mary for our nursing Mother? Fulfil this boast in yourselves; prove to the world that you are following no false teaching, vindicate the glory of your Mother Mary, whom the world blasphemes, in the very face of the world, by the simplicity of your own deportment, and the sanctity of your words and deeds. Go to her for the royal heart of innocence. She is the beautiful gift of God, which outshines the fascinations of a bad world, and which no one ever sought in sincerity and was disappointed. She is the personal type and representative image of that spiritual life and renovation in grace, "without which no one shall see God". "Her spirit is sweeter than honey, and her heritage than the honeycomb. They that eat her shall yet be hungry, and they that drink her shall still thirst. Whoso hearkens to her shall not be confounded, and they that work by her shall not sin."

—*Discourses to Mixed Congregations*

THE POWERFUL VIRGIN

This great universe, which we see by day and by night, or what is called the natural world, is ruled by fixed laws, which the Creator has imposed upon it, and by those wonderful laws is made secure against any substantial injury or loss. One portion of it may conflict with another, and there may be changes in it internally; but, viewed as a whole, it is adapted to stand for ever. Hence the Psalmist says, "He has established the world, which shall not be moved."

Such is the world of nature; but there is another and still more wonderful world. There is a power which avails to alter and subdue this visible world, and to suspend and counteract its laws; that is, the world of Angels and Saints, of Holy Church and her children; and the weapon by which they master its laws is the power of prayer.

By prayer all this may be done, which naturally is impossible. Noe prayed, and God said that there never again should be a flood to drown the race of man. Moses prayed, and ten grievous plagues fell upon the land of Egypt. Josue prayed, and the sun stood still. Samuel prayed, and thunder and rain came in wheat-harvest. Elias prayed, and brought down fire from heaven. Elisha prayed, and the dead came to life. Hezekiah prayed and the vast army of the Assyrians was smitten and perished.

This is why the Blessed Virgin is called *Powerful*— nay, sometimes, *All*-powerful, because she has, more than anyone else, more than all Angels and Saints, this great, prevailing gift of prayer. No one has access to the Almighty as His Mother has; none has merit such as hers. Her Son will deny her nothing that she asks; and herein lies her power. While she defends the Church, neither height nor depth, neither men nor evil spirits, neither great monarchs, nor craft of man, nor popular violence, can avail to harm us; for human life is short, but Mary reigns above, a Queen forever.

To say that prayer (and the Blessed Virgin's prayer) is omnipotent, is a harsh expression in every-day prose; but, if it is explained to mean that there is nothing which prayer may not obtain from God, it is nothing else than the very promise made us in Scripture. Again, to say that Mary is the center of all being, sounds inflated and profane; yet after all it is only one way, and a natural way, of saying that the Creator and the creature met together, and became one in her womb; and as such, I have used the expression above. Again, it is at first sight a paradox to say that "Jesus is obscured, because Mary is kept in the background;" yet there is a sense in which it is a simple truth.

−Meditations on the Litany of Loretto
for the Month of May

HELP OF CHRISTIANS

Our glorious Queen, since her Assumption on high, has been the minister of numberless services to the elect people of God upon earth, and to His Holy Church. This title of "Help of Christians" relates to those services of which the Divine Office, while recording and referring to the occasion on which it was given her, recounts five, connecting them more or less with the Rosary.

The first was on the first institution of the Devotion of the Rosary by St. Dominic, when, with the aid of the Blessed Virgin, he succeeded in arresting and overthrowing the formidable heresy of the Albigenses in the South of France.

The second was the great victory gained by the Christian fleet over the powerful Turkish Sultan, in answer to the intercession of Pope St. Pius V, and the prayers of the Associations of the Rosary all over the Christian world; in lasting memory of which wonderful mercy Pope Pius introduced her title "*Auxilium Christianorum*" into her Litany; and Pope Gregory XIII, who followed him, dedicated the first Sunday in October, the day of the victory, to Our Lady of the Rosary.

The third was, in the words of the Divine Office, "the glorious victory won at Vienna, under the guardianship of the Blessed Virgin, over the most savage Sultan of the Turks, who was trampling on the necks of the Christians; in perpetual memory of which benefit Pope Innocent XI dedicated the Sunday in the Octave of her Nativity as the feast of her *august Name.*"

The fourth instance of her aid was the victory over the innumerable force of the same Turks in Hungary on the Feast of St. Mary ad Nives, in answer to the solemn supplication of the Confraternities of the Rosary; on occasion of which Popes Clement XI and Benedict XIII gave fresh honor and privilege to the Devotion of the Rosary.

And the fifth was her restoration of the Pope's temporal power, at the beginning of this century, after Napoleon the First, Emperor of the French, had taken it from the Holy See; on which occasion Pope Pius VII set apart May 24, the day of this mercy, as the Feast of the *Help of Christians*, for a perpetual thanksgiving.

—Meditations on the Litany of Loretto
for the Month of May

DEVOTION TO
THE BLESSED
VIRGIN

THE HEART OF MARY

In Jesus Christ is the fulness of the Godhead with all its infinite sanctity. In Mary is reflected the sanctity of Jesus, as by His grace it could be found in a creature.

Mary, as the pattern both of maidenhood and maternity, has exalted woman's state and nature, and made the Christian virgin and the Christian mother understand the sacredness of their duties in the sight of God.

Her very image is as a book in which we may read at a glance the mystery of the Incarnation, and the mercy of the Redemption; and withal her own gracious perfections also, who was made by her Divine Son the very type of humility, gentleness, fortitude, purity, patience, love.

What Christian mother can look upon her image and not be moved to pray for gentleness, watchfulness, and obedience like Mary's? What Christian maiden can look upon her without praying for the gifts of simplicity, modesty, purity, recollection, gentleness such as hers?

Who can repeat her very name without finding in it a music which goes to the heart, and brings before him thoughts of God and Jesus Christ, and heaven above, and fills him with the desire of those graces by which heaven is gained?

Hail then, great Mother of God, Queen of Saints, Royal Lady clothed with the sun and crowned with the stars of heaven, whom all generations have called and shall call blessed. We will take our part in praising thee in our own time and place with all the redeemed of our Lord, and will exalt thee in the full assembly of the saints and glorify thee in the Heavenly Jerusalem.

Truly art thou a star, O Mary! Our Lord indeed Himself, Jesus Christ, He is the truest and chiefest Star, the bright and morning Star, as St. John calls Him; that Star which was foretold from the beginning as destined to rise out of Israel, and which was displayed in figure by the star which appeared to the wise men in the East. But if the wise and learned and they who teach men in justice shall shine as stars for ever and ever; if the angels of the Churches are called stars in the Hand of Christ; if He honored the apostles even in the days of their flesh by a title, calling them lights of the world; if even those angels who fell from heaven are called by the beloved disciple stars; if lastly all the saints in bliss are called stars, in that they are like stars differing from stars in glory; therefore most assuredly, without any derogation from the honor of our Lord, is Mary His mother called the Star of the Sea, and the more so because even on her head she wears a crown of twelve stars. Jesus is the Light of the world, illuminating every man who cometh into it, opening our eyes with the gift of faith, making souls luminous by His Almighty grace; and Mary is the Star, shining with the light of Jesus, fair as the moon, and special as the sun, the star of the heavens, which it is good to look upon, the star of the sea, which is welcome to the tempest-tossed, at whose smile the evil spirit flies, the passions are hushed, and peace is poured upon the soul.

Hail then, Star of the Sea, we rejoice in the recollection of thee. Pray for us ever at the throne of Grace; plead our cause, pray with us, present our prayers to thy Son and Lord—now and in the hour of death, Mary be thou our help.

—Meditations and Devotions

LACK OF DEVOTION TO MARY LEADS TO LACK OF DEVOTION TO JESUS

It has been anxiously asked, whether the honors paid to the Blessed Virgin, which have grown out of devotion to her Almighty Lord and Son, do not, in fact, tend to weaken that devotion; and whether, from the nature of the case, it is possible so to exalt a creature without withdrawing the heart from the Creator.

In addition to what has been said on this subject, I would here observe that the question is one of fact, not of presumption or conjecture. The abstract lawfulness of the honors paid to the Blessed Virgin Mary, and their distinction in theory from the incommunicable worship paid to God, are points which are already well known. Here, the question turns upon their practicability or expedience, which must be determined by the fact whether they are practicable, and whether they have been found to be expedient.

First, I observe that to those who admit the authority of the Fathers of Ephesus, the question is in no slight degree answered by their sanction of the (*Theotokos*), or "Mother of God," as a title of Mary, and as given in order to protect the doctrine of the Incarnation, and to preserve the faith of Catholics from a specious Humanitarianism. And if we take a survey at least of Europe, we shall find that it is not those religious communions which are characterized by devotion towards the Blessed Virgin that have ceased to adore her Eternal Son, but those very bodies, (when allowed by the law,) which have renounced devotion to her. The regard for His glory, which was professed in that keen jealousy of her exaltation, has not been supported by the event. They who were accused of worshiping a creature in His stead, still worship Him; their accusers, who hoped to worship Him so purely, they, wherever obstacles to the development of their principles have been removed, have ceased to worship Him altogether.

Next, it must be observed, that the tone of the devotion paid to the Blessed Mary is altogether distinct from that which is paid to her Eternal Son, and to the Holy Trinity, as we must certainly allow on inspection of the Catholic services. The supreme and true worship paid to the Almighty is severe, profound, awful, as well as tender, confiding, and dutiful. Christ is addressed as true God, while He is true Man, and as our Creator and Judge, while He is most loving, gentle, and gracious. On the other hand, towards Mary the language employed is affectionate and ardent, as towards a mere child of Adam, although it is subdued, as coming from her sinful kindred. How different, for instance, is the tone of the *Dies Iræ* from that of the *Stabat Mater*. In all the Marian hymns, we have an expression of the feelings with which we regard one who is a creature and a mere human being; but in the many hymns to Christ, we hear the voice of the creature raised in hope and love, yet in deep awe to his Creator, Infinite Benefactor, and Judge.

—*Essay on the Development of Doctrine*

MARY IN THE SPIRITUAL
EXERCISES OF ST. IGNATIUS

The Exercises are directed to the removal of obstacles in the way of the soul's receiving and profiting by the gifts of God. They undertake to effect this in three ways; by removing all objects of this world, and, as it were, bringing the soul "into the solitude where God may speak to its heart;" next, by setting before it the ultimate end of man, and its own deviations from it, the beauty of holiness, and the pattern of Christ; and, lastly, by giving rules for its correction. They consist of a course of prayers, meditations, self-examinations, and the like, which in its complete extent lasts thirty days. These are divided into three stages,—the *Via Purgativa*, in which sin is the main subject of consideration; the *Via Illuminativa*, which is devoted to the contemplation of our Lord's passion, involving the process of the determination of our calling; and the *Via Unitiva*, in which we proceed to the contemplation of our Lord's resurrection and ascension.

No more need be added in order to introduce the remark for which I have referred to these Exercises; viz. that in a work so highly sanctioned, so widely received, so intimately bearing upon the most sacred points of personal religion, only a slight mention occurs of devotion to the Blessed Virgin, the Mother of God. There is one mention of her in the rule given for the first Prelude or preparation, in which the person meditating is directed to consider as before him a church, or other place with

Christ in it, St. Mary, and whatever else is suitable to the subject of meditation. Another is in the third Exercise, in which one of the three addresses is made to our Lady, Christ's Mother, requesting earnestly "her intercession with her Son;" to which is to be added the Ave Mary. In the beginning of the Second Week there is a form of offering ourselves to God in the presence of "His infinite goodness," and with the witness of His "glorious Virgin Mother Mary, and the whole host of heaven." At the end of the Meditation upon the Angel Gabriel's mission to St. Mary, there is an address to each Divine Person, to "the Word Incarnate and to His Mother." In the Meditation upon the Two Standards, there is an address prescribed to St. Mary to implore grace from her Son through her, with an Ave Mary after it.

In the beginning of the Third Week one address is prescribed to Christ; or three, if devotion incites, to Mother, Son, and Father. In the description given of three different modes of prayer we are told, if we would imitate the Blessed Mary, we must recommend ourselves to her, as having power with her Son, and presently the Ave Mary, *Salve Regina*, and other forms are prescribed, as is usual after all prayers. And this is pretty much the whole of the devotion, if it may so be called, which is recommended towards St. Mary in the course of so many apparently as a hundred and fifty Meditations, and those chiefly on the events in our Lord's earthly history as recorded in Scripture. It would seem then that whatever be the influence of the doctrines connected with the

Blessed Virgin and the Saints in the Catholic Church, they do not impede or obscure the freest exercise and the fullest manifestation of the devotional feelings towards God and Christ.

—*Essay on the Development of Doctrine*

GOD ALONE—THROUGH MARY

Now it must be observed that the writings of St. Alphonsus, as I knew them by the extracts commonly made from them, prejudiced me as much against the Roman Church as anything else, on account of what was called their "Mariolatry;" but there was nothing of the kind in a particular copy that was sent to me. After inquiring, I was told that there certainly were omissions in one Sermon about the Blessed Virgin. This omission, in the case of a book intended for Catholics, at least showed that such passages as are found in the works of Italian Authors were not acceptable to every part of the Catholic world. Such devotional manifestations in honor of our Lady had been my great *crux* as regards Catholicism. I say frankly, that I do not fully enter into them now. I trust I do not love her the less, because I cannot enter into them. They may be fully explained and defended; but sentiment and taste do not run with logic: they are suitable for Italy, but they are not suitable for England.

But, over and above England, my own case was special; from a boy I had been led to consider that my Maker and I, His creature, were the two beings, luminously such, *in rerum naturâ*. I will not here speculate, however, about my own feelings. Only this I know full well now, and did not know then, that the Catholic Church allows no image of any sort, material or immaterial, no dogmatic symbol, no rite, no sacrament, no Saint, not even the Blessed Virgin herself, to come between the soul and its Creator. It is face to face, "solus cum solo," in all matters between man and his God. He alone creates; He alone has redeemed; before His awful eyes we go in death; in the vision of Him is our eternal beatitude.

Solus cum solo: I cannot completely recall what I gained from the Volume of which I have been speaking; but it must have been something considerable. At least I had got a key to a difficulty. In these Sermons there is much of what would be called legendary illustration, but the substance of them is plain, practical, awe-filled preaching upon the great truths of salvation. What I can speak of with greater confidence is the effect produced on me a little later by studying the Exercises of St. Ignatius. For here again, in a matter consisting in the purest and most direct acts of religion,—in the colloquy between God and the soul, during a season of recollection, of repentance, of good resolution, of inquiry into vocation,—the soul was "sola cum solo;" there was no cloud interposed between the creature and the Object of his faith and love. The command practically enforced was, "My son, give Me thy heart." The devotions then to angels and saints as little interfered with the incommunicable glory of the Eternal, as the love which we bear our friends and relations, our tender human sympathies, are inconsistent with that supreme homage of the heart to the Unseen, which really does but sanctify and exalt, not jealously destroy, what is of earth.

I am not sure that I did not also at this time feel the force of another consideration. The idea of the Blessed

Virgin was as it were *magnified* in the Church of Rome as time went on,—but so were all the Christian ideas; as that of the Blessed Eucharist. The whole scene of pale, faint, distant Apostolic Christianity is seen in Rome, as through a telescope or magnifier. The harmony of the whole, however, is of course what it was.

—Letter to Dr. Pusey

CONCLUSION: THE WOMAN OF THE APOCALYPSE

"A great sign appeared in heaven: A woman clothed with the Sun, and the Moon under her feet; and on her head a crown of twelve stars. And being with child, she cried travailing in birth, and was in pain to be delivered. And there was seen another sign in heaven; and behold a great red dragon ... And the dragon stood before the woman who was ready to be delivered, that, when she should be delivered, he might devour her son. And she brought forth a man child, who was to rule all nations with an iron rod; and her son was taken up to God and to His throne. And the woman fled into the wilderness."

Now I do not deny of course, that under the image of the Woman, the Church is signified; but what I would maintain is this, that the Holy Apostle would not have spoken of the Church under this particular image, *unless* there had existed a blessed Virgin Mary, who was exalted on high, and the object of veneration to all the faithful.

No one doubts that the "man-child" spoken of is an allusion to our Lord: why then is not "the Woman" an allusion to His Mother? This surely is the obvious sense of the words; of course they have a further sense also, which is the scope of the image; doubtless the Child represents the children of the Church, and doubtless the Woman represents the Church. This, I grant, is the real or direct sense, but what is the sense of the symbol under which that real sense is conveyed? *Who* are the Woman and the Child? I answer, they are not personifications but Persons. This is true of the Child, therefore it is true of the Woman.

But again: not only Mother and Child, but a serpent is introduced into the vision. Such a meeting of man, woman, and serpent has not been found in Scripture, since the beginning of Scripture, and now it is found in its end. Moreover, in the passage in the Apocalypse, as if to supply, before Scripture came to an end, what was wanting in its beginning, we are told, and for the first time, that the serpent in Paradise was the evil spirit. If the dragon of St. John is the same as the serpent of Genesis, and the man-child is "the seed of the woman," why is not the woman herself she, whose seed the man-child is? And, if the first woman is not an allegory, why is the second? if the first woman is Eve, why is not the second Mary?

But this is not all. The image of the woman, according to general Scripture usage, is too bold and prominent for a mere personification. Scripture is not fond of allegories. We have indeed frequent figures there, as when the sacred writers speak of the arm or sword of the Lord; and so too when they speak of Jerusalem or Samaria in the feminine; or of the Church as a bride or as a vine; but they are not much given to dressing up abstract ideas or generalizations in personal attributes. This is the classical rather than the Scriptural style. Xenophon places Hercules between Virtue and Vice, represented as women; Æschylus introduces into his drama

Force and Violence; Virgil gives personality to public rumor or Fame, and Plautus to Poverty. So, on monuments done in the classical style, we see virtues, vices, rivers, renown, death, and the like, turned into human figures of men and women. Certainly, I do not deny there are some instances of this method in Scripture, but I say that such poetical compositions are strikingly unlike its usual method. Thus, we at once feel the difference from Scripture, when we betake ourselves to the Pastor of Hermas, and find the Church a woman; to St. Methodius, and find Virtue a woman; and to St. Gregory's poem, and find Virginity again a woman. Scripture deals with types rather than personifications. Israel stands for the chosen people, David for Christ, Jerusalem for heaven. Consider the remarkable representations, dramatic I may call them, in Jeremiah, Ezechiel, and Hosea: predictions, threats, and promises, are acted out by those Prophets. Ezechiel is commanded to shave his head, and to divide and scatter his hair; and Ahias tears his garment, and gives ten out of twelve parts of it to Jeroboam. So too the structure of the imagery in the Apocalypse is not a mere allegorical creation, but is founded on the Jewish ritual. In like manner our Lord's bodily cures are visible types of the power of His grace upon the soul, and His prophecy of the last day is conveyed under that of the fall of Jerusalem. Even His parables are not simply ideal, but relations of occurrences, which did or might take place, under which was conveyed a spiritual meaning. The description of Wisdom in the Proverbs and other sacred books has brought out the instinct of commentators in this respect. They felt that Wisdom could not be a mere personification, and they determined that it was our Lord. The later-written of these books, by their own more definite language, warranted that interpretation. Then, when it was found that the Arians used it in derogation of our Lord's divinity, still, unable to tolerate the notion of a mere allegory, commentators applied the description to the Blessed Virgin. Coming back then to the Apocalyptic vision, I ask, If the Woman ought to be some real person, who can it be whom the Apostle saw, and intends, and delineates, but that same Great Mother to whom the chapters in the Proverbs are accommodated? And let it be observed, moreover, that in this passage, from the allusion made in it to the history of the fall, Mary may be said still to be represented under the character of the Second Eve. I make a farther remark: it is sometimes asked: Why do not the sacred writers mention our Lady's greatness? I answer, she was, or may have been alive, when the Apostles and Evangelists wrote—there was just one book of Scripture certainly written after her death, and that book does (so to say) canonize and crown her.

But if all this be so, if it is really the Blessed Virgin whom Scripture represents as clothed with the sun, crowned with the stars of heaven, and with the moon as her footstool, what height of glory may we not attribute to her? and what are we to say of those who, through ignorance, run counter to the voice of Scripture, to the testimony of the Fathers, to the traditions of East and West, and speak and act contemptuously towards her whom her Lord delighted to honor?

—Letter to Dr. Pusey